Understanding NLP

SECOND EDITION

Understanding NLP

Strategies for
better workplace
communication...
without
the jargon

NEILSON KITE AND
FRANCES KAY

KoganPage

LONDON PHILADELPHIA NEW DELHI

First published in Great Britain and the United States in 2009 by Kogan Page Limited
Second edition 2012

120 Pentonville Road	1518 Walnut Street, Suite 1100	4737/23 Ansari Road
London N1 9JN	Philadelphia PA 19102	Daryaganj
United Kingdom	USA	New Delhi 110002
www.koganpage.com		India

© Neilson Kite and Frances Kay, 2009, 2012

The right of Neilson Kite and Frances Kay to be identified as the authors of this work has been asserted by them in accordance with the Copyright, Designs and Patents Act 1988.

ISBN   978 0 7494 6381 6
E-ISBN   978 0 7494 6382 3

British Library Cataloguing-in-Publication Data

A CIP record for this book is available from the British Library.

Library of Congress Cataloging-in-Publication Data

Kay, Frances, 1949-
   Understanding NLP : strategies for better workplace communication– without the jargon / Neilson Kite, Frances Kay. – 2nd ed.
      p. cm.
   Includes index.
   ISBN 978-0-7494-6381-6 – ISBN 978-0-7494-6382-3   1. Neurolinguistic programming. 2. Business communication.   I. Kite, Neilson.   II. Title.   III. Title: Understanding neurolinguistic programming.
   BF637.N46K39 2011
   158'.9–dc23   2011022303

Typeset by Graphicraft Limited, Hong Kong
Printed and bound in India by Replika Press Pvt Ltd

Contents

About the authors vii

Introduction 1

PART ONE
A new way of understanding NLP 5

01 NLP building blocks 7

02 NLP beliefs simply explained 16

03 The mind and its effects on your behaviour 37

04 The body and its impact on communication 56

05 How your nervous system prepares you for anything 67

06 The incredible power of language 73

07 Rapport: your most important communications tool 92

08 Influencing skills are better than status 112

09 Learning: the most effective ways to do it 121

PART TWO

NLP and 26 situations or challenges you may face   133

10   Facing management challenges   135

11   Opportunities for personal development   158

12   Specific skills and capabilities to widen your range   175

Where to find out more about NLP and NLP facilities   214

Glossary   216

Further Reading   219

Index   220

About the authors

Neilson Kite studied NLP principles to develop a simple guide to Linguistic Psychology. His ability to demystify jargon is a result of his having had three careers: teacher of English in the United Kingdom and Sweden; manager, businessman and director of a number of knowledge industry companies; marketing consultant, mentor, coach and trainer in management and communication techniques. He has been widely published in the media on business topics and recently undertook groundbreaking work for the UN's International Trade Centre and the European Union. He is a regular speaker at national and international conferences on management, marketing and communication topics.

Frances Kay acts as a consultant to specialist firms, assisting them in establishing and developing corporate networks and relationships for their business development. With many years' work experience covering politics, the diplomatic service and law, the majority of her time is now spent writing, researching, editing and giving talks based on her book topics. With twenty books published to date, her area of expertise is career management and self-development. Frances is editor of *The Good Non Retirement Guide 2011*, and the author of *Successful Networking*, also published by Kogan Page.

They are the authors of *Understanding Emotional Intelligence*, also published by Kogan Page.

Introduction

An easier way to understand Neuro-Linguistic Programming

Neuro-Linguistic Programming, or NLP as it is more familiarly known, provides a powerful decoding mechanism for the way people speak, write and behave. Its purpose is to improve our understanding of what makes us and others 'tick' and it uses specific techniques to help us adapt our behaviour in pursuit of the results we want. It can remove mismatches between what people think, say, and do, and their genuine intentions.

Through understanding NLP beliefs and aligning ourselves with the reality of situations we encounter, there are immense gains to be made in the achievement of personal and workplace success. Many people say that NLP has transformed theirs and others' lives.

The specific objective of this book is to make NLP more readily accessible for anyone in a working environment so that they will immediately be able to apply its principles to achieve personal and organizational goals. A further objective is to do so in a language (and to describe situations) that are likely to be familiar to readers.

NLP applies to interpersonal relationships, in the boardroom, in management, selling, service, administration, caring for customers, negotiating, problem solving and indeed all aspects of working life. Its principles also apply to domestic relationships.

The starting point is not the vocabulary of NLP but real life people and situations that you are likely to recognize. NLP thinking is then applied to these situations. The reason for this itself reflects an NLP principle of learning. It is easier to attach a new meaning to a familiar object than to derive and remember meaning from something that is unfamiliar.

NLP is practised on five continents, hundreds of books have been written about it and hundreds of thousands of people have qualified as practitioners. Despite its exceptionally powerful attributes, it suffers, notably in the boardroom and other business environments, through having developed a somewhat inaccessible vocabulary of its own. As a relatively new area of study, it has developed its own distinctive characteristics and culture but represents a far too useful opportunity for personal and organizational development to be even partly obscured by its labelling and jargon. Hence this book.

However, in order to keep faith with those who have continuously developed NLP thinking and those who are curious about what vocabulary could apply in specific situations, a glossary has been included.

Background to NLP

Neuro-Linguistic Programming was invented by two academics in the early 1970s – hence the technically coined and rather cumbersome name. It was the brainchild of John Grinder, a professor of linguistics, and Richard Bandler, who studied psychology and psychotherapy. NLP developed from Grinder and Bandler investigating the work of outstanding therapists with a view to passing on their wisdom and techniques to others. It also included the study of hypnotherapy as a powerful tool in observing and resolving hidden psychological issues in people needing help.

The 'Neuro' in the name refers to the activity of the brain and of the nervous system. 'Linguistic' refers to the way we use words, the perceptions they create in people, and the interaction with the external world generally. 'Programming' is the process by which we choose and develop the way we think, use words, and harness our emotional senses in order to achieve our goals.

Scope of this book

The contents of this book are essentially about everyday life, particularly as it applies in the workplace. It does not cover therapy, hypnotism or those aspects of psychology better covered by more eminently qualified practitioners. Rather than provide an exhaustive analysis of an infinitely wide subject, it seeks to cover a comprehensive variety of situations, using them as analogies or templates that can then be applied universally to others. The intention is that you will recognize these situations as being familiar and then use that thinking to develop solutions to others.

The topics covered will provide insights into management issues, interpersonal differences, bullying, team performance, objective setting, the use of language, written documents, running meetings, selling and negotiation, influencing skills, dealing with difficult ideas, teaching, presenting, interviewing, motivation and many more.

You will find that NLP provides clarity and guidance for you, for others and for your organization in a remarkably simple and commonsense way. Everything has an explanation that NLP will enable you to understand better.

Everyone can achieve exceptional results

An important part of our consulting and coaching work has always been to encourage people. We help them discover that they have the capabilities and inner resources necessary to find solutions to problems. In many cases they far exceed their own expectations. Once they realize that they possess such strengths they usually achieve exceptional results – both for themselves and for their organizations. The process is then to convert belief into the use of words and behaviour that produce effective outcomes. For us, NLP has added a fresh dimension to the process of bringing out the best in people. It has helped bring clarity and focus to many different types of challenges and pointed the way to their resolution.

We have used NLP in practice for years and it has been proven to work over and over again. You too may have been using some NLP techniques and processes without knowing it. Once you realize the extent of the NLP 'toolkit' and understand the opportunities it gives, you will be able to make radical changes in the way you approach people, life and work. NLP enables you to address hundreds of different situations in ways that were previously unavailable.

The biggest hurdle to understanding and learning NLP principles and techniques has been the often tortuous vocabulary that has developed with it. Our aim was to change this in favour of everyday (well, almost everyday) language. We hope that you, the reader, will benefit from this new understanding. Our objective is to provide you with faster access to some really practical and powerful NLP thinking.

Part One
A new way of understanding NLP

Chapter 01
NLP building blocks

NLP is a model that can be used to understand patterns of thought, behaviour and language and to translate what you observe into methods of achieving specific outcomes. Those outcomes can be about you and your development, about other individuals, about the development of organizations and about learning and education.

NLP is a huge subject that is much written about and studied. To make it easier to digest, it has been broken down into its main components and principles summarized as follows:

1 Operational principles.

2 NLP beliefs simply explained.

3 Influences on the way you think and react.

4 NLP basic techniques.

5 Rapport: the key to successful personal communication.

6 The main differences between the conscious and unconscious mind.

7 Language and its vital role in written and verbal communication.

8 NLP as an aid to learning in others and in self.

Operational principles

These provide an evidence-based, practical route to achievement and include:

- knowing specifically what you want to achieve – a vision;
- knowing how you want to get there – a strategy;
- modifying behaviour in order to achieve the desired outcome – variation and best choice of tactics;
- taking immediate and positive action towards achieving the vision.

Applying these operating principles requires an attitude that focuses on aspirations, innovation and success as compared merely to the resolution of problems. In other words, what works for people is a positive mindset that expects rather than just hopes to achieve the outcome.

Being able to visualize the outcome provides a powerful incentive to achieve it. Prioritization of objectives and actions will make the process more efficient.

NLP beliefs simply explained

NLP embodies a number of beliefs and assumptions on which its philosophy is based. These are generally referred to as presuppositions and can vary according to different strands of NLP thinking. Rather than list these assumptions in the conventional way, they are first listed here and then in the next chapter, 'NLP beliefs simply explained', represented in the form of real-life situations with which we can all associate. The main beliefs and assumptions are:

1 People are not their words and behaviour.
2 Context is what determines others' interpretation of any action or communication.
3 Mind and body are inextricably linked.

4 A positive intention motivates every behaviour.

5 Actions do not necessarily represent intentions.

6 People will usually select what they believe to be the best choice.

7 Two people will see the same thing in entirely different ways.

8 People respond in accordance with their own interpretation of reality.

9 If you always do what you always did, you will always get what you always got.

10 Success depends on varying what you do until you get the result that you want.

11 People with the greatest choice and flexibility of behaviour come out on top.

12 Modifying your own behaviour can make others change.

13 It is impossible not to communicate.

14 The meaning of your communication is reflected in the response you receive.

15 People have all the resources they need; it is just a question of applying them.

16 Understanding comes with experience and is what enables you to explain something well.

17 Don't think 'failure', think 'opportunity to learn'.

18 There are no resistant audiences, just inflexible communicators.

The above beliefs and assumptions will give you a basis from which to observe your own and others' behaviour when faced with different people and situations. You can then, drawing on your own experience, apply NLP principles and techniques to create the best outcomes.

Influences on the way you think and react

The way people think and their reactions to situations depend on a number of factors, some of which are external and some internal. External factors include:

- your environment (which could include workplace, domestic, recreational, natural or public space);
- others' behaviour (and apparent emotions);
- others' words;
- others' physical characteristics;
- others' apparent motives and intentions.

Internal factors include:

- your role, identity and capabilities in the context of a particular environment or situation;
- your beliefs and values;
- the purpose you have in mind;
- your perceptions and preconceptions;
- your own emotional response to a person or situation.

Nothing is really as it is, only as we see it. Others' 'maps of the world' will be different. In influencing and being influenced by others, NLP says that you have to take all the above into account when choosing how to interact.

NLP basic techniques

- People can condition themselves to handle fear, anxiety and stress, for example, through making an association with something, possibly unrelated, that will calm them. NLP calls this fixation on a specific image, word or behaviour, anchoring.

- Similarly, you can discipline yourself and others to see things in a different context. This is a process of 'reframing' that better suits the outcome you want.

- Modelling is a core NLP process and skill by which you emulate another person's successful thinking, behaviour and approach so as to improve your own likelihood of success.

- Developing rapport through mirroring others' speech patterns and behaviours creates the opportunity to lead them where you want them to go and is a well-practised technique when you want to sell or persuade.

Rapport: the key to successful personal communication

> It takes just seconds to decide whether you like someone or not

It takes just seconds to decide whether you like someone or not, so managing that first impression is an essential step towards building the rapport that is so necessary for successful human interaction. Good rapport is essential for successful meetings, negotiations, appraisals, presentations, interchanges of information, and of course going on a date.

Mirroring someone else's words, tone and body language helps to establish rapport but is not the same as mimicry. You do not have to seem exactly the same as, but rather complementary to the other person.

Allied to rapport is the sense that once two people are in harmony, one of them can take the lead in something. This is why it is so important in a selling or negotiating environment where the purpose of an interaction is a specific, predetermined outcome as shown in the 'operational principles' above.

Although establishing rapport is not always easy, it can be immediately recognized when it exists between people. Their bodies, attitudes and tone of voice will seem synchronized. They will be relaxed and at ease with each other. If one or other is taking the lead, it will be done so harmoniously.

The main differences between the conscious and unconscious mind

The unconscious mind can deal with substantially more information than the conscious mind, which, it is generally believed, can cope concurrently with no more than seven items.

Because of the limited capacity to absorb data, the conscious mind is selective about what it does absorb. The way it selects is based on how the mind has previously been conditioned through influences such as the environment, specific incidents and other factors. In summary, the conscious mind:

- selects from a range of sensory information and converts it into thought;
- processes thought;
- comprehends numbers and symbols;
- analyses the situation;
- decides what strategies to adopt based on own capability;
- translates thought into language and behaviour;
- controls emotions.

The unconscious mind:

- influences emotional response;
- invokes spontaneous reaction (such as with phobias);
- preconditions conscious thought processes;
- unconsciously applies memories and experiences;
- picks up hidden signals;
- determines personality.

Language and its vital role in written and verbal communication

The psychology of language is fundamental to an understanding of what the NLP model represents. Language can be used both to clarify and to obscure truth. It can be used to encourage positive outcomes for all parties resulting from a piece of communication, or it can be used to manipulate the outcome in one side's favour. It can be at the same time very powerful and very inadequate in its ability to influence change.

Understanding the role and effect of language enables NLP to be applied as probably the most powerful tool you can use to achieve the outcomes you want in your working life. Poor communication can cause serious blockages to progress in an organization and is often used to prevent rather than enable change. Good communication has the effect of uniting people towards a common purpose and can never be overdone.

NLP postulates that there is a stratum of language that overlays other language in often unhelpful ways. In other words it can disguise the intent behind the language used in a particular situation. A classic example is 'I'd better let you get on then', which is more often than not a coded way of saying 'I want to finish this conversation'.

In receiving information, individuals delete from their minds what they are unable or unwilling to handle. This may be an unconscious reflex based on preventing the brain overloading, or a conditioned response based on, for example, a dislike of real or implied criticism.

Alternatively, if you do not unconsciously or consciously delete incoming information to your brain, you may instead distort it. In simple terms this can mean getting (deliberately or otherwise) the wrong end of the stick.

In addition to deletion and distortion is generalization, a facility that can be either useful or inadequate. Saying that you like fish is a generalization that conveys a useful message to someone who has invited you to dinner and wants to avoid giving you something you don't like. Saying that you like fish but not relating it to any context means very little.

When people want to win an argument and/or deny others a legitimate riposte, they frequently use techniques against which it is very difficult to compete. This is because you cannot argue logically against a case that was not based on logic or real evidence in the first place. Some of these false positions are shown below:

- Assertion versus argument: common in particular among politicians, who use such phrases as 'I know that it's the right thing to do for the country' without giving evidence to back the statement up.

- Falsely quote other authorities or unverifiable statistics to reinforce your own position: 'The supervisor doesn't want me to let you do it', or 'Three-quarters of staff don't want that to happen.'

- Give people a choice that denies a middle option: 'You are either for us or against us.'

- Argue from ignorance: 'We cannot have evolved from other primates because...'

- Question the other person's motives even though you cannot know what they really are: 'You're just saying that because...'

- Appeal to popularity: 'We're absolutely committed to your well-being and development' (when there's clear evidence to the contrary!)

- Tell transparent lies: 'The cheque will be in the post to you next week.'

- Use loaded language: 'When are you going to improve your time-keeping?'

- Imply guilt: 'Don't you want to save the starving children of the world?'

> the words we use only represent a small fraction of what we are really thinking

Generally speaking, the words we use only represent a small fraction of what we are really thinking. NLP enables you to distil and interpret what is really meant.

NLP as an aid to learning in others and in self

The best aids to learning are wants, needs, necessity, fun and curiosity. If we think of the circumstances in which young children most quickly learn things, food (and its availability) is a strong influence, as is a parent's touch and the stimulation of emotions through sounds and pictures.

NLP embraces different types of learning whether through association and habit, or trial and error. In acquiring a skill there are various steps to go through until the skill becomes a habit. In the process there will inevitably be mistakes, without which the lessons will not have been comprehensively learned. NLP's operational principles revolve around adapting to circumstances in order to be able to achieve the specific outcome you want. In effect, NLP's success comes from openness to a learning process.

In teaching others, or more correctly in allowing them to learn, you apply a variety of strategies that lead to a discovery process that they might not have instigated on their own. The strategies include tapping into natural curiosity, creating stimuli through incentive and reward, and eliciting a change in perspective compared to the way they usually view the world.

The NLP belief is that if you always do what you always did, you will always get what you always got. The brain has to be exercised and stretched in order to improve its fitness and performance.

Chapter 02
NLP beliefs simply explained

In order for NLP to have a practical use there needs to be a sound basis by which language and behaviour can be judged. NLP principles are therefore based on a set of underlying beliefs or assumptions (often called presuppositions) about human characteristics and capabilities as well as the process and meaning of communication.

Below are illustrations about people, their perceptions, emotions, behaviour and language together with an NLP rationale for explaining them. Different NLP sources quote different sets of beliefs, of which there are more than 20. These are the 18 most generally relevant.

These assumptions enable you to assess your own and others' thinking and behaviour in any given situation. In recognizing the truth and familiarity of these scenarios, you will then have a more memorable and readily available means of applying your own NLP analysis and response.

People are not their words and behaviour

Just as someone who 'gets it wrong' is not a bad person, someone who 'gets it right' is not a good one. Words and behaviour are only a temporary representation of that person at that time. Who they are is in a totally different context. The world is full of people who have been misjudged for whom they really are.

CASE STUDY   Nelson Mandela

Probably the best modern example is Nelson Mandela, imprisoned as an 'enemy of the state' by the South African government for 27 years, yet eventually celebrated by the population and the rest of the world as the nation's saviour. It was his words and behaviour that resulted in his imprisonment, yet his values and wisdom that now transcend that narrow perception.

It must be tempting for schoolteachers to label their more unruly pupils as lost causes when the challenge is not what you as a teacher can tell (or teach) them but how they can discover the other valuable choices available to them. It would be erroneous to think that pupils' behaviour needs to be 'repaired' when it is their existing energies that, of their own volition, could be channelled differently. The successful teacher is the one who facilitates the process of learning and transition rather than just 'bangs heads together'.

NLP asserts that corrective action against the individual or the organization is less powerful than facilitating growth and development. As Winston Churchill once said: 'Don't teach me, let me learn.'

Context is what determines others' interpretation of any action or communication

How often have you misinterpreted someone else's intentions? It can be a common cause of anger, fear, surprise, embarrassment or laughter.

CASE STUDY

One couple tells the story of visiting the manse to discuss arrangements for their impending marriage. The minister held out his hand which the wife-to-be shook warmly. When she realized that the hand had been outstretched to take her coat, not to shake her hand, she had an uncontrollable bout of giggling and the minister just looked uncomfortable. Had he added the words 'Shall I take your coat?' the outstretched hand would have been in an unambiguous context.

Take an entirely different scenario. If someone you don't know walks towards your house at the dead of night carrying a chainsaw, you have every right to feel apprehensive. If a man you have asked to cut down a tree walks towards your house with a chainsaw in the middle of the day, you will probably be pleased that he has arrived to do it.

If you have an important visitor to your office and you ask a colleague to make some coffee for you both, the chances are that you will get a frosty response unless you have taken the trouble to pre-arrange it diplomatically. He or she, and this is a common situation, may think their status has been undermined.

From the three illustrations above, NLP assumes that it is the context of an action and not the action itself that gives it its meaning. The Ronnie Barker hardware store sketch where there was verbal ambiguity as to whether the buyer wanted 'four candles' instead of 'fork handles' further illustrates the point. The context only became clear when he said, 'handles for forks'.

If you consider the sentence 'You're coming home with me to-night', it entirely depends for its meaning on the tone you use and on which word you put the main emphasis. If you don't know the context, you don't know the meaning.

Mind and body are inextricably linked

The way a person thinks affects how they feel. The condition they are in physically affects how they think. Mental attitude affects your body and it is possible to make a change in one and affect the other. It is now medically proven that the immune system is linked to brain activity, so if you are suffering from stress your health will deteriorate. When you have a positive mental outlook your body will be stronger and healthier; you will look and feel good.

If you're caught on the hop one day and need to dash to the local shop to buy necessities, you'll be in a rush, casually dressed, hair tousled and not looking your best. You'll keep your head down, avoiding people's eyes. The chances are that you'll bump into someone who knows you. Don't be surprised if they enquire after your health. Now you may be in the peak of condition, but if your appearance belies the fact, the likelihood is that your friend won't believe you. Body language reveals everything.

> Body language reveals inconsistencies that can then be questioned.

At work, however, this could be quite significant. If you have a colleague who suffers from mental stress, not only is their performance in the office below standard, but they probably also have poor physical health and don't look well. The mind–body connection is closely integrated. Neurotransmitters are chemicals that transmit impulses along the nerves, and it is through these that the brain communicates with the rest of the body.

A positive intention motivates every behaviour

Sometimes people behave badly to make themselves feel better. This is often difficult to understand from an objective viewpoint.

CASE STUDY

A bright new employee was asked by his boss to give a presentation to his department. He was naturally quite nervous but the information he produced was important and the facts and figures he presented were accurate. Because his presentation lacked confidence (due to inexperience, not low intellect) the manager told the young man his performance was poor. He added that perhaps, despite his good qualifications, he wasn't up to the job he was doing.

This behaviour was as unkind as it was unhelpful. The boss seemingly had no excuse for such conduct. Naturally the new employee on the receiving end was upset. But the explanation behind the manager's offensive manner was that he felt threatened by the newcomer's intelligence and qualifications. The manager's own insecurity made him behave in a bullying way. By belittling a subordinate, the nasty boss felt he would gain some self-esteem.

All actions have at least one purpose: to achieve something that is of value or gives benefit (to the person exhibiting the behaviour) however bad or unwarranted that behaviour might be. People who act in this way can only feel 'big' by making someone else feel 'small'.

In NLP it is important to remember that a person is not their behaviour, and that the behaviour they exhibit will not necessarily have positive benefits for anyone other than them. Once you understand that the reason why a person behaves in a negative way towards others is to get a positive result for himself, your flexibility of mind increases, which helps you communicate better.

Actions do not necessarily represent intentions

CASE STUDY

It was widely reported in the press that when Cherie Blair, the former UK prime minister's wife, said to Princess Anne that she could call her Cherie, Princess Anne responded that she was not brought up to do that sort of thing. Cherie Blair's action had a positive intention and would have been appropriate in a context other than communicating with a member of the Royal Family. Similarly, a junior member of staff kissing the chairman's wife on the cheek, although it would have been appropriate if she were his aunt, would not usually be considered proper etiquette, however well intentioned.

CASE STUDY

A specific example from the world of direct marketing was a campaign prompted by a managing director asking, 'Could we not have a bit more cheesecake [sic] to spice up our [technical] message?' The result was an expensive photography shoot of a suggestively clad model posing in front of a computer. The resulting photograph was cut into four strips, each one of which, starting from the top of her body, was to be mailed on successive weeks. The strap line was, 'XYZ Services – only part of the picture'. Unsurprisingly, there were some strongly worded complaints.

In each of the above illustrations, behaviour, as is all behaviour, was based on positive intentions but ill-judged actions. The NLP assumption is that all behaviour is appropriate in some context but not in all contexts.

People will usually select what they believe to be the best choice

CASE STUDY

Mary was anxious to impress her dinner guests. When shopping she bought the most expensive items she could afford: fine wine, filet steak and luxurious chocolate for dessert. After her last party everyone had raved about the excellent food and said what a great hostess she was. She prepared the meal with care to offer her guests. One of them was driving, so he could not drink the fine wine and had to drink water. Another was a vegetarian, so she could not eat the steak and ate only salad. The third was allergic to chocolate and missed out on the pudding. Mary was disappointed that her dinner party was a failure after she had tried so hard. Each of her guests was embarrassed and disappointed that her choices were so limited from their own perspective.

When a person has a better choice of behaviour that also achieves their positive intention, they will usually take it. Mary bought the best items she could afford, hoping to give her guests a treat. She was tempted to repeat a pattern of behaviour because it had worked for her previously. Yet under different circumstances (a person who had to drive, a vegetarian and someone allergic to chocolate) it was disastrous. The guests could have told Mary about their circumstances, or Mary should have checked with them first. Context makes meaning – but context is a matter of perception. Inappropriate behaviour in a set of circumstances may simply be the result of misinterpreting the context.

The saying 'The road to hell is paved with good intentions' applies here, and explains why one person's best choice often seems a poor choice to someone else.

Two people will see the same thing in entirely different ways

If you told your great-grandmother that someone was 'gay', she would immediately conjure up a picture of a happy, lively person. If you said the same thing to today's generation, the word would immediately be associated with sexual orientation. Our interpretation is based on individual knowledge and experience, rather than the word itself.

If you show someone a swastika, it depends on their circumstances whether they see this as a negative symbol of the Nazi movement or an important symbol or design used for hundreds of years in the Hindu, Buddhist and Jain religions.

The map of the London Underground bears no resemblance to the real routes and distances that trains actually travel. It is a representation that has the purpose of making it quicker to locate routes and destinations, and making it easier to travel. Even geographically accurate Ordnance Survey maps do not depict the real picture of the territory they cover.

It is the brain that constructs any individual's picture of the world and this is frequently evident in the workplace when, for example, what someone writes or says may be interpreted in diametrically opposite ways. 'I'll hang up now and let you get on with your work' could be seen as being considerate. On the other hand, it could be interpreted as someone's impatience to end the conversation.

NLP believes that people's interpretation of words, maps, gestures and symbols is inevitably based on individual experiences, learned responses, memories and beliefs; in other words, their perception. As with a map, a human's ability quickly to absorb all the information contained on it is severely limited and therefore the brain makes a perceptual précis and not a literal translation. No one can change the objective truth, but people can and should be prepared to modify their own perspective in the interests of getting the most positive outcome.

People respond in accordance with their own interpretation of reality

It is impossible to guarantee the weather in the United Kingdom because of our changeable climate, and it often rains. Yet someone who always carries an umbrella or takes a raincoat with him when he goes out could be considered by many to be weird, obsessed about the chances of getting wet. If this person had a history of chest infections and feared catching a cold could lead to serious complications, he would not want to run the risk of getting soaked to the skin. What might seem odd behaviour to some people can be perfectly logical to others if you know what is in their mind.

CASE STUDY

A woman who attended her local church was difficult to talk to and always presented as an 'angry' person. She did not communicate easily and few people attempted to approach her. She had had a difficult personal life and was scared of making friends in case she was 'let down'. One day another member of the congregation invited her to a party. When she got to the house she saw a beautiful grand piano and asked if she could play it after supper. What transpired was a superb recital by an accomplished classical pianist. It was an evening to remember, and the woman was a different person once someone had uncovered her gift.

In NLP thinking, you respond according to the map you have in your head (perception). That map is based on what you believe about your identity, values, attitudes, memories and past history. Some maps work well in situations where others don't. You can't possibly know what map other people hold in their heads. It is best to be tolerant and understanding of situations and people even when you don't comprehend them, because you could be missing out on something valuable and enriching. The more flexible your map becomes, the greater freedom and better experiences you will have.

If you always do what you always did, you will always get what you always got

The human race has survived and evolved because of its ability to adapt to circumstances. People who can adapt to the circumstances in which they find themselves will be more successful than those who cannot adapt. The same is true for companies and organizations as for individuals.

CASE STUDY

A marketing company with an impressive client list and a distinctive competitive edge could never enjoy consistent, exponential growth because it was limited by its ability to forecast business performance accurately beyond just a few months. It relied for many years on short-term sales projections and could not therefore plan and budget accurately for the business. Recognizing that by carrying on doing the same thing, performance would remain static, the company brought in a new managing director with particular strengths in planning and forecasting. The result was a dramatic improvement in performance and the ability to make longer-term growth decisions as a result of the directors' newly found confidence. It was the preparedness to change that made the difference.

Although you may become frustrated that things always turn out to be the same, despite a mindset that says change is very difficult, there are always choices and good ideas you've not yet thought of, despite indications to the contrary.

The misanthropic Mr Scrooge from Charles Dickens's *A Christmas Carol*, having realized the effect of his attitudes and actions, discovered, through changing himself, a well-being that had previously eluded him. Most people have experienced others, often customers, whose demeanour seems permanently grumpy and who wonder why people try to avoid contact with them. It is not for us to cope but for them to change; but importantly, we should also try to change our own attitudes to them in order to give them a reason to do so.

Governments go through a cycle that sees them popular at first, with that popularity waning after a period. A frequent cause of their becoming unpopular is an insistence on sticking to the same agenda in spite of changing circumstances in the world around them. Those that can adapt are more likely to last longer.

NLP believes that it is how we respond to the world around us that determines our success. Adapting to circumstances is more effective than trying to impose our control on them.

Success depends on varying what you do until you get the result that you want

This is a learning process, the old 'trial and error' method of achieving your outcome. It is well illustrated by experiments that were carried out many years ago on rats, which had to negotiate a maze before reaching the food that they could smell at the other end. By trying different routes, eliminating the dead ends and progressively memorizing the right set of trails, they were eventually able to reach the food every time without taking a wrong turn.

Examples of this can be seen in sport when, in order to win a match, different strategies are tried until the most effective is identified and then vigorously applied. A tennis player might, for example, experiment by playing more frequently on an opponent's backhand, slowing a service so as to be more accurate, approaching the net more frequently, using drop shots or trying lobs. If you do not vary your tactics and insist on playing the same game you will not win the match.

> NLP is all about changing thinking and behaviour in order to increase the likelihood of success.

NLP is all about changing thinking and behaviour in order to increase the likelihood of success. An additional NLP tenet is that you can learn by emulating others' successful actions and that this can be a highly effective route to achieving successful change for yourself or your organization. You do not have to be perceptually limited by your own resources.

People with the greatest choice and flexibility of behaviour come out on top

Have you noticed how the most successful of politicians achieve, initially at least, such wide appeal? Most possess a broad set of communications tools, including seriousness, humour, appealing for sympathy and support, appearing to listen, being indignant or angry and, of course, kissing babies. They know how to work a crowd, to act sincerely when the situation demands and smile at the right times. The less successful politicians find it harder to apply such a range of techniques to the different situations in which they find themselves.

Leaders are, on the whole, comfortable in anyone's company and will as easily speak to postmen as presidents. They have a wide choice of behaviours that can be used to suit different occasions.

In the world of work, people often feel limited in their choice of career progression because they lack the skills, knowledge, experience and qualifications to do what they really want. The problem here is that they are limited by their own beliefs. It is not necessarily that they do not have confidence in their own ability, but that they fear others will not find them believable. The reality is that we all have the resources in us to do what is necessary to achieve our goals, but may need to change our attitudes and behaviours in order to give ourselves a wider choice of routes to success. In the case of people with apparently limited career horizons, if they realize that acquiring new skills and knowledge is easier once you adapt your mindset, they can open up a whole range of opportunities that were not previously available.

Advertising agents and designers often make a pitch to their prospective clients based on a choice of three options. They argue that if they come up with just one creative solution they risk the choice between a 'yes' and 'no' answer and may possibly lose the business. If they come up with two solutions they put the client on the horns of a dilemma and this could delay the decision-making process, arguing the pros and cons of what seems an evenly balanced case for both. Through offering a choice of three, it is much easier to decide.

The irony of this, however, is that the agency probably has its own preference for what it thinks is the best one of the three, but the client will quite often choose one of the others contrary the expert's view of design and communications logic.

NLP assumes that the more choice we have, the easier it is for us to take control.

Modifying your own behaviour can make others change

If you can change yourself you can effect a change on the people around you. Scientifically speaking, if one element in a system changes, then the whole arrangement alters to incorporate that modification.

CASE STUDY

Jack hated the mornings; it was a stressful time for all and often led to arguments, tantrums and tears. His wife and children made him late leaving the house almost every day because they were never up in time. The breakfast routine was chaotic and he usually arrived at work frustrated and angry. He also felt guilty that he hadn't the time to say goodbye and have a nice day to his family whom he adored. Sarah, his wife, was an owl (up late in the evenings) while Jack was a lark (no problem getting out of bed early). He decided to rise an hour earlier each morning to get himself ready for work before the rest of the family woke up. This small change in his own behaviour wasn't difficult as he was playing to his own strength (early rising). Within a few weeks he noticed that the whole atmosphere in the family was much calmer, particularly in the mornings. His wife, he realized, had changed her routine. Sarah, utilizing her owl strengths, had decided to spend the hour before going to bed getting ready for the morning. She laid the breakfast, got the children's school clothes and lunches prepared in advance. The result of one person's ability to change just a little, was a calmer happier family with a workable weekday routine.

The NLP assumption here is that you can change your circumstances by changing yourself, rather than expecting or demanding that other people make a change. The bonus is that if you can achieve a personal shift of attitude, behaviour, belief or value, you will have an effect on those around you: family, friends, work colleagues, etc.

It is impossible not to communicate

If someone does not reply to your letter or return your phone call, you usually assume one of three things: the letter or phone call was not received, the person is away or you have been impolitely ignored, at least for the moment. The latter feeling is what is inevitably communicated when you do not receive your reply, although nothing has, in fact, been communicated at all.

CASE STUDY

At a meeting of four people to discuss some project issues and the way forward in an IT project, one of the attendees spent the first 20 minutes with head and eyes down, writing occasionally in a notebook on his knee and seemingly ignoring the other three in the room. The person who called the meeting became increasingly agitated at this apparently non-cooperative stance until, towards the end of the meeting, this 'rude' colleague came up with a well-thought-out solution to all the issues that needed to be covered. He brought immediate clarity to the discussion and enabled the meeting to be brought swiftly to a conclusion. Through not communicating he had communicated lack of involvement, when the opposite was true.

In negotiations about a worldwide distribution deal, the company wanting the licence did not communicate for several days despite having expressed extreme urgency to sort things out quickly. Although this eventually turned out to be for technical reasons, the product owners who stood to be paid for the licence believed that it was a negotiating ploy and lost faith in the good intentions of the potential partner, thus prejudicing the deal. Lack of apparent communication can have a powerful effect.

Relationships between couples can often be punctuated by what seem to be deliberate silences. It is assumed that these silences are deliberate, but it may be that one person's thoughts are miles away trying to sort something out, or it could be that umbrage has been taken about a previous comment. Because no one provides a context for these silences, a whole variety of messages may be wrongly communicated.

'I have nothing to say on that matter' can communicate volumes about what a person really thinks. It is seldom taken literally. Shy people, through not communicating, communicate shyness. Trappist monks observing a vow of silence communicate their beliefs and values. Silence in a room can indicate respect. It all depends on the context. NLP thinking addresses non-communication as a valid part of the communications process.

The meaning of your communication is reflected in the response you receive

> The message you transmit may not be the same one that is received.

There are no failures, only responses and feedback. If you aren't getting the result you want, change what you are doing. You may be perfectly clear in your own mind what you mean, but the interpretation and response that you get will reflect the effectiveness of your communication. The message you transmit may not be the same one that is received.

CASE STUDY

There is the apocryphal story of the troop commander preparing to go into battle and requiring backup.

A messenger was sent to Headquarters who reported the following to the General: 'Send three and four pence, I'm going to a dance.' The General dismissed the messenger and ignored the seemingly trivial request. A catastrophic defeat followed. What the commander had actually said was: 'Send reinforcements, I'm going to advance.'

People can only respond to what they think is meant.

CASE STUDY

A girl sent her friend the following text message about meeting at the theatre to see a play: CU 7.30. The friend arrived at the theatre at the appointed time to find that the play had started, and subsequently missed half the performance. The girl was furious that her friend hadn't bothered to turn up on time for a special treat. The sender of the message had meant 'Curtain Up at 7.30'. Her friend had interpreted the message as 'See You at 7.30'.

In NLP, if you want people to respond appropriately to what you're saying, pay great attention to the whole communication when transmitting and receiving. Flexibility in the way you communicate eliminates misunderstandings. Remember it's not just the words, but the non-verbal clues as well. You want to avoid being as frustrated as the lecturer, who was overhead to say: 'I know you heard what I said, but did you understand what I meant?'

People have all the resources they need; it is just a question of applying them

If you do not speak Swedish, but need to in order to undertake an overseas project, then you are perfectly capable of learning it. You may not even know how you would set about it or how long it would take, but you certainly have the resources to find out. You have already learned your own language, so you do not need to seek out special learning skills as it is obvious that you have the capability of learning a language.

CASE STUDY

A long time ago, a nine-year-old who was sent away to boarding school after the premature death of his father decided that he would run away, and managed to travel by train from East London to Southampton with just sixpence (old money) in his pocket. This was not enough to cover the fare from Snaresbrook to Waterloo, let alone from Waterloo to Southampton. When told at the Snaresbrook station that sixpence was not enough, he asked where sixpence would get him and was told Charing Cross on the other side of the River Thames. He could walk across Waterloo Bridge to Waterloo Station. By one means or another he managed to board the Southampton train and eventually to get home (only to be sent back the following day).

What this demonstrates is that with a goal in mind and even against the odds, we can apply hitherto unproven resources if we have the determination to do so.

In workplace situations we are capable, one way or another, of solving any problem put in front of us. If the metaphorical path is blocked by a tree, rather than assume that we have to remove the tree, we can alter our thinking to find ways of going round it. The resources we need could be both conscious and subconscious as well as behavioural. An NLP tenet is that we can apply our minds to make the changes and adjustments we need to be successful, provided we are focused, determined and the outcome is physically achievable. Having the will to do so is then the precondition for success.

Understanding comes with experience and is what enables you to explain something well

How does a male doctor explain to an expectant mother what she is going to experience during labour when she asks him if it will be painful? He has the knowledge because of his training and he can describe it theoretically, with eye-catching pictures perhaps, but only in words. Even midwives, who are specialists in such matters, if they are not mothers themselves, cannot know what it feels like to have a baby. Your understanding of something is clearly enhanced by your experience of having seen or done it before. You are therefore able to explain it from the perspective of that experience as well as your acquired knowledge.

It is far easier to describe something you're familiar with, whether you're explaining how you changed the flat tyre on your car beside the road in the dark yesterday evening, or describing the South American rainforests you've recently visited on vacation. You'll be able to do it in greater depth and detail and to be more convincing than someone who has seen a programme about it on television or read a book on the subject. Experience is unique to each individual. If you've seen, heard and felt something yourself, your ability to communicate this to others is greatest.

> Experience is unique to each individual.

When training people, it is best to do so from a point of experience, which is why it is so comforting to see on your first flying lesson that your instructor has a good few thousand hours recorded in his log book. In the workplace, the manager who has progressed his way from the lowest position in the company and has worked in a variety of jobs on his way up has the best skills for training his subordinates.

Don't think 'failure', think 'opportunity to learn'

Many people respond defensively to customer complaints but the more enlightened realize that they can be of real value to an organization. If you think of complaints as failure, your attitude to them will be different than if you think of them as an active way to become more effective in your customers' eyes.

Organizations can choose to handle complaints in a number of different ways. They can ignore them, respond defensively, send a standard response, or interact with the customer to understand the problem fully and pass the information into the management system as a means of ensuring continuous improvement. It is obvious that the first two ways are not productive. The third, sending a standard response, reduces the customer to a commodity and although some people think that the complaint has been dealt with, in reality it has not.

If you think you are 'rubbish' at something, then you probably are. If you think that there is probably a better way of doing things and change your approach in order to find it, you will then have used that experience as a means of personal improvement. There are no failures, only circumstances. You can choose how you wish to handle something and different people will handle different situations in different ways.

> There are no failures, only circumstances.

Some people, often not very good managers, will infer failure by the language they use. 'What went wrong then?' is a much less constructive question than asking 'How are we going to prevent that happening again?' Finding someone to blame, even if it is yourself, does not solve a problem and NLP postulates that there is no such thing as failure, only feedback.

There are no resistant audiences, just inflexible communicators

The precondition for good communication is to create the circumstance in which people will be receptive. It is easy to blame the other person or an audience when it may be the approach you have adopted that is the problem. You are in control of your own mind and therefore have a choice about how you communicate. It may be that you have not established sufficient rapport, or clarified the context of the communication. You may be inhibited by lack of belief in your ability to put something across.

Whatever the reason, you have an opportunity to do something about it. You may need to understand your audience better, to observe more accurately and to practise alternative communications skills based on the filters that people apply. You may be supplying information in too large chunks or you may be introducing detail that loses the reader or listener.

In NLP, if you can establish, through research and observation, the triggers for likely interest, the 'digestion' capability of the audience and their capacity to absorb information, then empathy and interest can more readily be established.

CASE STUDY

A company with a highly technical and complicated set of products recently set up what it called an 'incubator unit' of technical staff and managers. Its purpose was to propose new products and services that could be sold as having an impact on their clients' profitability. The objective was to come up with proposals that members of the sales force would embrace with enthusiasm, helping them sell more.

At a presentation, the orientation of the speakers was about the ingenuity of the new products and services proposed. The orientation of the audience was different. They were interested in how easy it would be to sell these products and services, and how much bonus they would earn as a consequence.

Had the speakers started with 'a fantastic opportunity for you to earn more money', an eager listening platform would have been established and they could have built on that interest. NLP says that the starting point of any communication is the state of mind of the recipient.

One successful salesman explained that his success in getting people on side was due to being a 'chameleon' – an entirely appropriate metaphor for NLP in action.

Chapter 03
The mind and its effects on your behaviour

Although mind, body and nervous system are indivisible parts of the whole person, they are treated separately so as to make it easier to reference particular aspects of each. Thus, the following three chapters look at how the mind works, how the body works in relation to the mind and how the nervous system affects physical state, action and response.

For NLP to be an effective tool in improving communication depends on opening your own and other people's minds. Everyone is conditioned by their upbringing, experience and learning to see the world in their own unique way. NLP aims to remove barriers and prejudices so that minds can converge and successful interpersonal transactions can take place. Shakespeare's sonnet 116 that starts 'Let me not to the marriage of true minds admit impediments' illustrates what could today be regarded as a prescient NLP principle.

Your mind affects your physical state and can be used to control it

If you know that you have to address an audience, however experienced you are, you will probably feel nervous, your heart will beat faster and you may perspire. This is despite the fact that you are clear as to what you will talk about, have sufficient knowledge to be credible and are adept at expressing yourself. You have consciously put yourself into a position in your terms where you expect success but also risk failure. Your body has made certain adjustments so that your capabilities have been heightened. More blood is being pumped around your circulatory system to your muscles and to your brain, in order to ensure performance. We need the stress in order to maximize our chances of success. A useful analogy is to think of a car's fan belt. If there is no tension between the pulleys it will not be effective. It needs just the right tension to operate at maximum efficiency. It will also not operate efficiently if the tension is too great.

Clinical trials that include placebos in the research process demonstrate unequivocally that if the mind believes a condition is being genuinely treated, a healing process can take place. Kissing a child better, as we all know, removes the sensation of hurt.

In the workplace there are many tensions and, these days, increasing levels of stress. If we think of stress as being a mismatch between perceived demands and a perceived inability to cope, we can understand how people become physically affected, feel lethargic and sometimes ill. When the mind is in a stressed state we also know that the body is more susceptible to real infection.

CASE STUDY

The UK's former deputy prime minister famously punched a man who had thrown an egg at him at close quarters. People said that it was a spontaneous reaction, and his 'boss' the prime minister explained it away by saying, 'That's just John'. NLP would argue that he chose to respond in that way.

> We all have control over the way we respond to events

We all have control over the way we respond to events, even though we may blame our conditioning for acting in a particular way. Consider, for example, what you would do if struck on the cheek by a one-year-old baby. The chances are that your reaction would be substantially different than if you were struck on the cheek by a 17-year-old youth. The thing that makes the difference is the context, so we do in fact make a mental calculation of that context in the split second before reacting. If a waiter accidentally spills soup on you in a restaurant,* you can choose whether you react angrily or calmly. It is not automatic that you need to feel angry.

NLP recognizes the potential physical effects of the mind on the body and provides the insights and mechanisms to capitalize on this, inducing the body into positive instead of negative states.

* See 'A soup story' in the 'You can control your mind and therefore your reaction to situations' section at the end of this chapter.

The mind retains certain types of information without even trying

It can sometimes be difficult to remember people's names or in what context you have met them before. It is not always easy to remember the words of a song, a speech, a piano piece, or a part in a play that you want to learn off by heart.

On the other hand, certain things stick in the mind without you trying. These include sounds, tunes, smells, physical sensations, images, and of course, words and phrases. We also more easily recall such things as rhyme and alliteration than ordinary prose.

As NLP is about our ability to communicate and to be communicated with, words and phrases play a very important part in conveying meaning and activating memory.

Why is it that so many people remember the line 'Friends, Romans, countrymen, lend me your ears' from Shakespeare's *Julius Caesar*? Or why do they remember UK prime minister Margaret Thatcher's remark about doing a 'U-turn' when she said 'You turn if you want to. The lady's not for turning!' The answer in both the above cases is that there is a twist. 'Lending ears' is a contradiction in terms. 'You turn' is a play on 'U-turn' and uses the

> We remember the incongruous more easily than the norm

same phonic to infer a totally different meaning. We remember things that cause a disconnection to the way in which we usually decodify language. In other words we remember the incongruous more easily than the norm.

Rhett Butler's final remark in the film *Gone With The Wind* was spoken by actor Clarke Gable and is still remembered over half a century later for its emphasis on what seems to be the wrong word. 'Frankly, my dear, I don't *give* a damn' sounds strange with the emphasis on 'give' and not on 'damn'. But everyone who has seen the film remembers it because of the unexpected emphasis that has been so widely and frequently referred to.

An open mind is the key to making progress

An open mind enables us to adjust more easily to circumstances and to the people around us. If the mind cannot adjust, then effective two-way communication is obstructed. You may, for example, find circumstances in your working life where you do not see eye-to-eye with colleagues and cannot see how to overcome the apparent impasse. There may be management blockages, difficult customers or unreliable suppliers getting in the way of what, in your perception, should be trouble-free progress.

The challenge is to clear yourself, or those you deal with, of what is in effect a limiting mindset. An important principle is to practise unconditional regard so that personal judgement does not get in the way of good interpersonal transactions. It is only through unconditional regard that full rapport can be established.

Inevitably, your mind will have been conditioned by your personal experiences, memories, values, peer group influences, culture and beliefs that have been built up over time. But recognizing that your own map of the world is different from everyone else's and moving towards someone else's, or at the very least a neutral position, is a prerequisite for communicating successfully. We say that people have rose-tinted spectacles or chips on their shoulders when describing those with whom balanced communication is difficult.

John O'Keeffe, in his book *Mind Openers for Managers*, says: 'we lose much of our potential through having a limited mindset'. He believes that you stick with a mindset to justify a position you have taken compared to someone else's, but that this inhibits creativity and the likelihood of arriving at a truthful outcome.

A simple illustration from his book shows that, in the absence of an obvious, simple solution, people tend to overcomplicate things. For example, most people when shown the sequence of letters O T T F F S and asked to say what the next two letters in the sequence are, will most likely find it a problem to identify the right solution. The tendency is to think of it as an acronym or phrase or saying with a logical ending – which it is not. If you did find the right solution, it should then be much easier to find the next two letters or pairs in the sequence N W R OU IV I, but for most people it still eludes them because this is not the way the mind is usually set.

When told that the first sequence is based on the first letters of numbers one to six, a very easy and logical answer, the solution becomes immediately apparent to everyone. They do not necessarily apply the same model or logic to the second sequence, even though it simply shows the middle letter or letters of those same words in the first sequence.

Another illustration of mindset rigidity is a combined alphanumeric test that asks you to:

1 Think of a number between 2 and 10.

2 Multiply it by 9.

3 Add together the two digits in the result.

4 Subtract 5.

5 Convert the number to a letter 1 = a, 2 = b, 3 = c and so on.

6 Think of a country beginning with that letter.

7 Take the second letter of that country and think of an animal beginning with that letter.

8 What colour is that animal typically?

Whatever the arithmetic, you will not be surprised that it automatically leads to one predetermined letter only. Most people will mention the country that first comes into their heads and, more often than not, the same country will be chosen by others as it has a comparatively high profile.

If you have done the above exercise, are you now thinking of a Danish grey elephant? That is what the majority will have concluded (with a couple of eels thrown in) as they are likely to have been conditioned by their learning experiences to think of Denmark and elephant first.

The NLP position is that there is always a mindset barrier to be overcome in any transaction (as illustrated by the 'mindset elephant'). By suspending your likely disbelief of the new and untested, and changing the way you are naturally inclined to think, creative solutions to problems will become much easier and you can achieve the best from the widest choice of strategies.

Your behaviour reflects both your conscious and unconscious states of mind

Your mind has both a conscious and an unconscious state, both of which have a bearing on how you behave and respond to the different stimuli around you. Your conscious mind enables you to think, apply logic, calculate, decide and send a signal to the body to take or avoid deliberate action. Your conscious mind also enables you to translate your thoughts into language and communicate accordingly. It enables you to convert what you sense through sight, hearing, touch, smell or taste into an appropriate meaning and to make conscious choices. However, because there is always more sensory information available to you than can adequately be absorbed and processed, the mind filters or summarizes that which it can consciously handle. As everyone is different, this forms their unique map of the world. It may or may not be a good representation of reality. Nonetheless it is *your* reality and the one that you will have to adjust when communicating with others and their different maps.

Your unconscious mind is conditioned and characterized by subliminal experiences. These include irrational fear or dislike (such as of harmless spiders), muscle memory (where your fingers automatically hit the right keys on a keyboard or you can ride a bike, for example), and inexplicable pleasure (such as from taste and music). It is also made up of instinct as well as forgotten incidents and experiences that may have affected your life in the past.

Your values, beliefs and intentions are embodied in both your conscious and unconscious mind, as is your reactive and proactive behaviour. If you have an ingrained aversion to men with beards, or women with beards for that matter, you may be conditioned by both a conscious and unconscious reaction when meeting them.

Your mind is also affected consciously and unconsciously by such stimulants as alcohol, where 'beer goggles' distort how you think and behave, but not necessarily who you are. Some believe that drink reveals the real person, thus the expression *'in vino veritas'*, which loosely translated means 'when people drink wine they reveal the truth about themselves'.

How incompetence can lead to competence

Both conscious and unconscious states of mind can be altered through learning. This is well illustrated through the example of someone learning to drive. When you are planning to have your first driving lesson, you are not conscious of how incompetent you are. You have no idea what you have to do or how to do it. You are 'unconsciously incompetent'. As soon as you have been shown how to operate brakes, pedals, steering wheel, gears and mirrors, you are then conscious of your lack of skills in coordinating their use. You have become 'consciously incompetent'. After several lessons you can be trusted to drive the car, albeit in a faltering way. You can then be said to be 'consciously competent'. You know what to do but still have to think about it while you are doing it. After a while, steering, gear changing and braking are done subconsciously as you have acquired the driving 'habit'. You are now 'unconsciously competent'. The footnote to this is that when you have become unconsciously competent, it is then that you begin to develop bad habits such as steering with one hand, using rear view mirrors insufficiently, speeding and so on. In an ideal world you would need to relearn good habits and repeat the cycle.

NLP suggests that the conscious mind can deliberately and directly affect the unconscious mind, but this view is contested in some circles. In the illustration above it can be seen that, through learning, good and bad habits can be acquired over time and that the deliberate process of learning will lead to unconscious activity in the brain. Where there is less evidence is in the cases of hypnotism and, unfortunately, torture, where there is clearly an effect on someone's persona but that cannot as yet be scientifically quantified.

The rules by which you run your life comprise both conscious and unconscious elements. Your values may be those you were taught by your family or they may have been influenced in the opposite direction because of your wish to be different. If one of your 'drivers' is punctuality, or honesty, it will probably influence you for life. If you are perpetually late or economical with the truth, you will always have that tendency, even though you can consciously modify your behaviour to change that impression. If you have a tendency to be competitive you will permanently remain so unless your unconscious mind can be altered in some way.

As well as values, some of your competencies are unconsciously permanent. You never, for example, forget how to ride a bike, apply lipstick without a mirror or do up your shoelaces.

In dealing with others, NLP says that you should always be aware how powerful the unconscious mind is in regulating everyone's life, and take account of unconscious as well as conscious effects. Hypnotherapy and other means of trance induction are used by many NLP practitioners to probe and affect the unconscious mind. The aim of this book, however, is not to argue the merits of this but to provide a practical toolset for our self-development and better communication with others.

People are different and respond to different approaches

Although we receive information through all our main senses – sight, sound, taste, smell and feeling – people mainly process information in a preferred style based just on sight, sound or feeling.

Seeing

There are those who respond best to visual stimuli, those who respond best to words and sounds, and those who respond to feeling. In the latter case, that feeling can be in either the tactile or the emotional sense.

If you want to inform or influence visually inclined people, their minds will respond well to pictures, diagrams and visual demonstrations. This can also include analogies where a representative picture in the mind can convey the sense of a meaning: 'It's as easy as shelling peas', for example, or more graphically still, 'Think of the world as an orange.' Visual people tend to think easily in pictures and will readily superimpose the alternative one you give them.

Visually inclined people will tend to use vocabulary related to seeing: 'Yes, I see that', 'It's looking good', 'Do you see what I mean?' and so on.

Hearing

By contrast, the sound-orientated person picks up on words, nuances of tone, pace, volume of delivery and the logic of language and rhetoric. This is as well as being particularly influenced by music and other evocative sounds such as applause, or even the memory of someone's voice from years ago.

Those for whom sound is the primary influence might say: 'I like the sound of that', or 'I hear he's a bit of a rogue', or 'Let's hear what she has to say.'

Touching and feeling

Touching is an essential part of communication and conveys both sensory and emotional information. Touch provides essential comfort and assurance to babies, as does hugging someone when they are upset. Emotion can also be stimulated by what we see and hear and can be both positive and negative. We speak of 'touchy-feely' people and associate them not just with physical contact but also in terms of their emotional orientation.

People for whom touch and feelings are their most dominant communication influences might say: 'I feel it's time to move on', or 'I really don't like his attitude', or 'What does everyone feel about that proposal?' or 'I love that idea.'

The above orientations are predominant thinking styles and not of course rigid. You may find yourself applying all three at different times and in different circumstances. If you want to improve communications effectiveness in yourself, then establishing rapport by addressing people in the way that most suits them will help to get the message across. If you are addressing an audience and its different mindsets it is useful to deliberately include visual, auditory and emotional stimuli to ensure that the right information has been absorbed.

You can choose between negative and positive thinking

NLP recognizes that if you are to be successful you need an aim and a strategy to achieve that outcome. The same applies just as much to organizations as individuals. Either you have an inclination to embrace challenges or you find ways of avoiding them. The positive mindset thinks in terms of goals to be achieved, whether that is in terms of material acquisition, overcoming physical obstacles, attaining excellence, improving relationships and so on. The negative mindset is often triggered by a problem – the avoidance of failure, the fear of impending debt, embarrassment if you do not deliver something on time.

If you have a positive mindset, this will be reflected in your vocabulary, your tone, your body language, approachability and general demeanour. You will tend to appreciate things, to take trouble and to encourage others.

If your orientation is negative, you are more likely to use negative language that anticipates problems more than have the expectation of success. Negative thinking is sceptical, critical, pessimistic and sometimes cynical. If your direction of travel is towards a clear goal, you are likely to be more successful in life than if you wait to see what the world throws at you. The widely used analogy is that positive people see the glass as being half full, while negative thinkers see it as half empty.

> If your direction of travel is towards a clear goal you are likely to be more successful in life

In an interview situation, you may be asked the question: 'Why do you want to leave your current job?' If you are an achievement-orientated person you will say something positive about your ambitions or the attractiveness of the position on offer. If you do not have such positive thoughts you might say something about the current position not being interesting or challenging enough. In the former case you would be attractive to an employer. In the latter, doubt about your attitude would be raised in the discerning interviewer's mind.

How your ego directly affects others

NLP calls on various manifestations of psychology including Freudian thinking on ego states. The hypothesis, in simple terms, is that at any given time we are all in (or in and out of) one of three ego states. These are nominated as Parent, Adult and Child and relate to any of the 'transactions' that we have with another human being. The system is called Transactional Analysis as it analyses what is going on when two people interact.

One of the easiest ways to summarize the effects of these ego states is to consider the interaction between real parents and their children. If, for example, you as a parent tell your 13-year-old daughter to go and tidy her bedroom, the chances are that you will get one of two responses. Either she will complain and display predictably negative body language or she will acquiesce quietly and go and do it. If you are, or have been, the parent of a 13-year-old daughter, you will know which outcome is the more likely.

In that same scenario, if you as the parent receive a negative response, there's a fair chance that you will become cross and complain, maybe along the lines of: 'I'm fed up having to go on at you all the time. I've got better things to do with my time', and so on. If that is the case, you have transferred from your Parent ego state into a Child ego state. You have emotionally internalized the problem.

Ironically, at that point the daughter could conceivably say: 'Oh all right then, don't worry about it Mum (or Dad), I'll go and sort it if it makes you feel any better.' She has transferred from her original Child ego state into that of a Parent offering a practical solution 'As long as you get off my back.'

The Parent and Child ego states can vacillate between two people but usually, as long as they do, it is difficult for a smooth 'transaction' to take place. The better solution is for the two parties to be in the neutral Adult ego state.

Parallel scenarios to this can happen in a work environment, and a key skill is in recognizing what is going on and leading the conversation on to productive neutral (Adult) ground. This can be a product of changing what you do or say to establish the rapport through which you can then lead the other person to where you want both of you to go. Such techniques are frequently used, for example, in a sales environment to overcome sales resistance where an individual may be trying to exercise control because of a fear that he or she needs to resist the seller.

In a different context, some leaders are criticized, and often not much respected, because people think they are power-mad manipulators. However talented and skilful they may be in their own right, they are unable to establish relationships of mutual respect and people may even fear them.

An inflated ego will make it difficult for an egoist to see what is apparent to others. They will not trust the person with a different view even though he or she does have merits in a particular argument.

These people are, in fact victims of their own egos and not the winners that they would like others to believe. Successful people, however, have no need to victimize others or themselves. The NLP principle is to recognize and abandon personal 'baggage' and realize that the winning strength of really effective people is their humility and ability to transact with everyone. It is all in the mind.

Controlling your own attitudes will help you control situations

After the first physical impression, attitude is the biggest determinant of others' response to you. It is the reason people hire you, marry you, divorce you and take notice (or not) of what you stand for. This means opening your mind and practising the unconditional regard referred to earlier. Attitude is entirely in the mind, though it can manifest itself through many different behaviours and choice of language.

NLP therefore assumes a number of things that should be taken account of when faced with people who do not have the same view of the world that you do. Although it is extremely difficult, and takes practice to swallow your preconceptions, in order to get into others' minds, it is important to take on board the following:

- There are no difficult people – they are just 'different' people.
- There are no irrational people, just those who see things differently.
- People always try to do their best to address or cope with any situation.
- The flexibility of your own behaviour will give you the best means of influencing others.
- We cannot influence people unless we listen and understand.
- People will from time to time change their position and can be influenced to do so.

Others' minds, when they do not wish to cooperate, will lead them to display, for example, bullying tendencies, to adopt specific postures, to be completely inflexible or to be apathetic.

Bullying can take many forms. It does not have to be aggressive and is equally damaging to an interpersonal transaction as quiet sarcasm or mockery. Whatever it is, it undermines the other person's position. Posturing aims to establish such a superior position as cannot easily be challenged. Inflexibility is a rigid refusal to cooperate and apathy a powerful tool that can completely de-energize the other person.

> We cannot influence people unless we listen and understand

The essence here is that he or she is trying to exercise control or, at the very least, trying to avoid your control. In some senses this is a positive state, which is a lot better than no state at all because, in the final analysis, you can do something to change it.

Your NLP challenge is to recognize what state is being displayed and devise a strategy, through adapting your own state, to alter theirs and open them up to proper communication. To do this you will have to separate facts from feelings and find a way for them to do the same.

A key factor here is that your behaviour is not necessarily the real you, so analysing someone's underlying values and beliefs will make them more susceptible to accepting that there are different realities that could be considered.

Finding out a bit more about yourself

Based on Ingham and Luft's Johari Window model is the presupposition that all of us possess both known and unknown qualities. Added to that, with the right stimulus, we and others can find out more about us than is currently known. With this knowledge comes the opportunity to capitalize on or suppress those things that affect our interaction with others. The model shows that:

- There are open characteristics that are evident both to others and ourselves.

- There are things that others perceive in us of which we ourselves are unaware.

- There are things we know about ourselves but others do not.

- There are hidden things about which neither we nor others have any awareness.

FIGURE 3.1 How the Johari Window model works

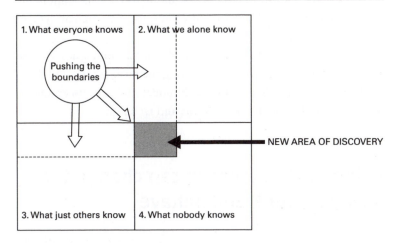

Based on Figure 3.1, it can be seen that by using observation and analysis we can push back the common borders of square 1. By doing so we automatically increase levels of awareness in ourselves and others, even to the extent of finding out things about us that are new to everyone.

Implications on a wider scale: marketing and branding

The art of marketing is to get into and influence the minds of people collectively. 'Winning mind-share' is a frequently used marketing expression. It is also said that it is 'better to be first in the mind than first in the marketplace.' To this extent, similar rules apply when personally persuading individuals or captive groups (in the sense that they belong to an organization or common interest group) where similar mental filters or emotional patterns are in place and need adjusting in order that messages will be positively received.

NLP is looking for common ground between a leader and a follower in order to achieve a positive outcome for both parties. Marketing is exactly the same. Branding is only different in that it is planting seeds and not direct propositions. In effect, branding is establishing a form of rapport, while marketing is stimulating desire, reinforcing preferences and calling for a particular type of response.

Branding, if you will, is like the smile that accompanies a warm greeting. Marketing is about stimulating the business in hand. Both marketing and branding fit the NLP model and are susceptible to the use of similar psychological tools and techniques.

Being part of a group can change the way you think and behave

What you think, and therefore the way you behave, is different when you are alone compared to when you have others around you. A principal contributor to this is your awareness of your status within the group and the impression you want to make on it. It is as if the influence of a group can put you into a suspended state of mind; in other words, a kind of trance.

When involved in a group on some task or project with which you are familiar, the likelihood is that you and your senses will be stimulated by that group to perform better. However, if within that group you are exposed to unfamiliar ideas and less comfortable challenges, the likelihood is that you will perform less well. Self-consciousness impairs the ability to think and act in a totally relaxed way.

It is well known that groups can talk themselves into extreme positions. Fascist, fundamentalist and revolutionary ideologies typify the power of groups that are united by common beliefs. A characteristic of such groups is that they are able to stifle dissent as their members are prepared to subjugate any doubts they have for the common good of the group as a whole. On the other hand, groups divided by internal differences will lack the ability to act with the same power as cohesive ones. A highly focused group can be an immense force for good as well as for negative purposes.

If you have ever tried to recruit a new honorary treasurer or secretary to a club or association, you will be aware that group participation does not easily stretch as far as a queue of willing volunteers for these positions. Members of the group generally like being members but can be considered inherently averse, lazy or apathetic when asked to take direct responsibility for outcomes. Passivity can ultimately be harmful as it can allow the dynamics of a group to be left to a minority and the group eventually to radicalize or fail.

This 'bystander effect' can also be seen in situations where, for example, if someone was being robbed in front of others, the group effect could mean no one going to help. This would be despite the fact that most individuals, if present on their own, would be inclined to assist in some way. The more people there are around it seems, the less likely it is that someone will offer help.

In NLP terms, people are programmed in different ways according to the circumstances in which they find themselves. Group situations can only be changed through intervention and the use of leadership skills and psychology.

You can control your mind and therefore your reaction to people and situations

Have you ever watched someone behaving in an extremely angry way with someone else and then noticed that the same person can immediately switch to being nice to another person who happens to come along?

Have you also wondered why some people take offence at things, while others just take them in their stride? The fact is that you choose to take offence. It is not something that is thrust upon you.

Some people take offence as a means of exercising power and control. They take a particular ego position that directly diminishes the ego of the other person. Because people tend to think that anger or taking offence are spontaneous positions, they do not necessarily believe that they can do much about it. NLP would argue that there is a lot you can do to change someone's apparent emotional state.

CASE STUDY   A soup story

A few years ago at an office celebratory Christmas Dinner at which there were over a hundred guests, a young and obviously inexperienced waiter was clearing soup plates from the first course by placing empty soup dishes one into another. One of the guests had only half drunk the soup in his dish and the waiter placed the other dishes onto it.

The consequence was that the soup came gushing out at the sides. The waiter panicked and lifted the dripping dishes over the head of another guest, soaking his hair, jacket, shirt and tie.

Everyone expected an angry reaction but the incident was handled with complete calm. The judgement was that the waiter had not made the mistake deliberately, was fully aware of, and embarrassed by what he had done, and would never repeat the error.

No particular purpose would have been achieved through anger. The manager's offer to pay the dry cleaning bills and invite the guest back to other events free of charge was all that was needed to redress the situation, and everyone emerged wiser about the need for more thorough waiter training. The waiter himself would have learned more through embarrassment than being shouted at.

Anger can often cause resentment in return and does not recognize the best way to a positive outcome in this kind of situation. It may be appropriate in other contexts as a means of getting what you want, but is by no means the involuntary reaction that some people suppose.

An NLP operating principle is that you have choices in the way that is best to achieve your outcome and may have to vary your thinking and behaviour to achieve it.

Chapter 04
The body and its impact on communication

NLP and body language in general

The body is the physical part of the Mind, Body and Nervous System. It is the bit you can see, hear, touch and smell. In other words you can get to grips with it in a more tangible way than the mind and nervous system. Your state of mind powerfully affects your physical state, so it helps if you can be in control of your body. It makes situations more controllable when your body works for you, not against you.

The effect of the nervous system on the body is explained in the following chapter. The nervous system exerts an enormous influence on your body and determines how it responds to different situations. It triggers both your unconscious and conscious responses. The somatic nervous system coordinates voluntary body movements (those activities that are under conscious control) and the autonomic nervous system is responsible for coordinating involuntary functions (such as breathing and digestion). The involuntary responses are more difficult to control because they are impulsive. This is because they are reactive, designed to protect you from danger (for example, fight or flight mechanisms). If someone looks as if they are about to attack you, you can't afford to use valuable time thinking about what to do next when you should be beating a hasty retreat.

In NLP, being aware of what your body is doing is hugely important. It is also a great advantage to be able to read the signals from other people. Communication is, after all, a two-way process and NLP is one of the greatest aids to good messaging.

The way your body behaves is your most potent asset in many situations. Body movement and language figure significantly in any context. Don't forget that one of the NLP beliefs is that it is impossible not to communicate. NLP helps you learn how you can use your body to obtain the greatest effect – even if it means that you do absolutely nothing at all.

Our physiological make-up gives us a clue to the importance of body language. The Optic Nerve, the largest nerve in the body, is many times larger than that of the ear. People are thus far more likely to follow what you do than what you say. You can test this for yourself by saying to someone quickly 'Put your hand on your shoulder' yet simultaneously putting your hand on your head. Most people will put their hand on their head despite your instruction – and embarrass themselves in the process.

You can use body language to good and bad effect. A bully will use facial expressions and cast his eyes upwards if he wants to make you feel uncomfortable or inferior. On the other hand, someone who wants to make you feel good amplifies your feelings with a smile, welcoming gestures and open hands. That's all very obvious, of course, but the reason for considering it are to do with having a greater impact on others because you are conscious about how you can deliberately change the impression you make. This is really important in the context of persuasion. It is relevant, for example, in selling situations where you want someone to trust you, when you are negotiating something or asking for a concession – even, indeed, a pay-rise.

In essence, you can use body language to give yourself authority, command respect and get people to listen and act. Words alone will not be as powerful.

Your body language tools are your posture, your face, eyes, torso, hands, legs, feet and much more. Politicians are trained in such techniques with some being notably more effective than others. Recent world leaders make an interesting contrast in style. Success, as we often observe, is determined by demeanour and appearance compared with the content of their words.

If you want to appear more authoritative, raise your sternum (breastbone) by just an inch when addressing, for example, an audience. It will make you seem anchored and stronger. Plant your feet evenly and firmly on the ground and keep your eyes and chin up. It will be difficult to ignore you.

Use the palms of your hands in an open upward gesture to encourage an audience, whether of one or several. In contrast, use those hands in a downward fashion to subdue their expectations.

In meetings, remember that your legs can be a real give-away and a distraction to others. If you are feeling uncomfortable, keep your legs still. If you are standing, don't sway.

Your eyes are also really important. Eye contact is essential but not for so long that the person on the receiving end of your attention wonders whether you want to kiss them or kill them.

Interpreting others' body language can also be an acquired skill and enables you to be supportive or resistant – whatever seems to be in your best interests.

The interpretation and use of body language fit very well with NLP assumptions and development and enable you to strengthen the impression you create and the results you achieve.

Part 2 of this book describes actual situations and how to handle them. These relate mainly to professional or workplace situations where you are trying to communicate effectively with other people. But they are equally applicable to personal circumstances. Using your body correctly, harnessed to NLP thinking and behaviour, can change potentially disastrous encounters into win–win situations. The correct use of your body can also vastly improve inner confidence and self-esteem.

Two of the most useful NLP techniques where the body is concerned are modelling and mirroring. When you model your behaviour on someone else's successful conduct, you hope to achieve similar results. Even if it doesn't work immediately, you may significantly improve your chances of success the next time you behave in such a way. Everything in NLP gets easier with practice.

Where mirroring gestures are concerned, these are used mainly to create rapport with other people. This technique influences people to your way of thinking and works well in situations where you wish to negotiate, persuade or do business with someone.

Instant messaging

Everyone knows it takes only seconds to form a judgement about someone. Where professional dealings are concerned, however much you try to suspend reaction, you are likely to have an instant viewpoint – 'I like him', or 'Can she be trusted?' – when you first meet a person. Within a few moments, assumptions and judgements are made. People make a snap decision about someone because of the way they look, speak or how they present themselves.

Do you remember the well-documented statistics about making a successful presentation? Fifty-five per cent of the impression you make is how you look, your posture, gestures and what you wear; 38 per cent is the energy and enthusiasm, pace and tone of voice; and only 7 per cent is what is contained in the words you say to your audience.

As you can see, your words represent just the tip of the iceberg. Yet anyone giving a presentation for the first time usually worries continually about what they are going to say. Sometimes, if they are not being coached, rehearsed or mentored, they forget about everything except the words they are going to speak. Then they cannot understand when the event is a disaster. Why? It is a common enough mistake to make, and most people have committed such an error at least once in their career. Usually people learn from experience that if you pay attention to the bits you can see (the body) it can make all the difference between success and failure.

How you use your body is far more persuasive than what you say. Harness it to saying the right things (linguistic communication allied to positive body language) and you can

> How you use your body is far more persuasive than what you say

literally knock people's socks off. So rarely, though, do people realize the power that they possess. If you are lucky enough to be able to invest in presentation training, or your organization offers you the opportunity, do take it. It is not only very helpful in alleviating shyness and building confidence but it also incorporates some NLP skills training. To become adept at using NLP, you need practice, and one way of doing this is by learning presentation skills.

Presenting yourself in the best light

There are many expert tips on how to conduct yourself in public. Some presentation consultants start by making a video of the way you walk, talk, stand and sit, and how you conduct yourself at meetings or corporate events. This is a fairly harsh way of finding out what you don't do particularly well. But if you can bear to watch, it will help you sort out which bits of your bodywork need attention. Even if you don't have the opportunity to obtain professional assistance, there is a lot you can do to help yourself get to grips with your body and the language it conveys.

First of all, make a list of the areas you think need attention. This could be something like weak posture or negative body language. Ask a close friend or colleague what they think you are good at, and what areas perhaps they consider could be improved. Something as simple as slouching at your desk is a bad habit. Many people who have bad deportment just don't realize it. But it is usually very noticeable. It could affect (in a negative way) the way they react to you, or what they feel about how you do your job.

Think how much more positive an impression you give if you sit upright at your desk and look alert when people are passing. Imagine a 'golden thread' running from the top of your head to the ceiling. Whenever you stand or sit, imagine this thread pulling you upright. You will instantly grow taller and be more noticeable (in a positive way). Make sure your face is relaxed and, if you can manage it, give a smile. You have transformed yourself in one quick and easy step. The reaction of others will have changed towards you too, for the better.

Now, watch out for indicators of nervousness or lack of confidence. This could be evident in someone who fidgets, or clasps their hands tightly or keeps their head low to avoid eye contact. It is quite natural and instinctive when apprehensive to want to make yourself smaller. Crossing your arms or holding your bag or coat in front of you are other tell-tale signs. Anyone who has studied the effect of body language in a communication context will know that arm movements give powerful clues as to how confident, open and receptive you are. The more relaxed your limbs, the more confident you will appear. When everything is tightly clenched the effect is rarely reassuring to others present.

The more outgoing you are, you'll use your arms to great effect – with confident movements and gestures. If you're a quiet type, you will move your limbs less and keep them close to your body. It is quite interesting to watch old film footage of politicians when they first came to prominence. Look at how they change and develop as they gain experience in front of the camera. Did they learn it themselves, have they studied NLP or have they the benefit of coaching from PR professionals?

The body as an instrument

> using open body language
> will make you more
> credible and persuasive

When it comes to looking the part, if you want to be seen as a confident and self-assured person, capable of conducting business negotiations in a cool professional manner, using open body language will make you more credible and persuasive. Try standing upright, balancing on both feet with your weight evenly distributed.

Remember that your body is an instrument – it conveys emotion. But like any instrument, it should be smoothly played. There is nothing worse than cacophony.

Body language can be loud, it can be soft, but it should always be harmonious. It should also be appropriate to the situation. NLP states that success depends on varying what you do until you get the result that you want. Your body can do an infinite variety of things. It can also do nothing. The power of silence and remaining motionless is something that should not be forgotten. It can have a huge impact in certain circumstances.

When it comes to mirroring gestures, use them correctly. You are not mimicking someone (if they cough, you cough, etc). You are echoing their body language to reinforce the fact that you are empathetic towards them. It is one of the basics of NLP and a sound technique for creating rapport with anyone. By imitating what the other person does, it endorses the favourable view they've formed of you. It reinforces the right impression and creates a bond between parties at the outset.

If actions speak louder than words, listen to the volume of your body language. When you are trying to create a favourable impression with someone, your body will naturally point towards them – your face, hands, arms, feet and legs. These gestures can be quite subconscious, but they are picked up easily by the other person. It's something you've probably noticed dozens of times amongst people you've sat next to at work, or when travelling or in social situations. Next time you have an opportunity, watch how individuals position themselves when communicating with each other. They naturally angle themselves towards the person with whom they are trying to create a positive impression. Contrastingly they will turn away from those whom they are seeking to avoid.

Using your eyes to communicate

It is important not to underestimate the power of your eyes. The eyes are central in the communication and rapport-building process. Making appropriate eye contact in social situations or business dealings is vital and can make or break negotiations in some circumstances. You could be interacting with someone you don't know very well, so there are a number of things it pays to remember. It's quite natural to look at people from eye to eye and across the top of the nose. This is the safe area to which eye contact should be confined.

Eyes can be very expressive too. They can convey emotion and you can often tell if someone is being less than truthful by the way their eyes appear. If there is incongruence between what they are saying and how they look at you, be careful. It often pays to reserve judgement until you can get more information or are better acquainted with them.

Some people are so adept at communicating by eye contact alone that they hardly need to speak. Most of the time people are using multiple signalling methods, so it is easy to overlook things. Next time you have an opportunity, concentrate on someone's eyes to see what they are communicating to you. People who are hard of hearing watch lips and eyes as the main indicators of what is being communicated.

Should you be nervous it is easy to stare obsessively at someone when they are speaking. This is rather off-putting and a negative form of eye contact. The opposite end of the scale, looking away completely, slow blinking or closing the eyes for longer periods than normal, can indicate a lack of interest or even worse, boredom. None of these will help build rapport and would indicate that the NLP skills are in need of further practice.

A final word on the subject of eyes: if you point to something you want to draw attention to, the person you are talking to will usually lift their head and look towards that object. By engaging eye contact again afterwards it should reaffirm the emphasis of the meeting or exchange. Practise this once or twice to see whether it works for you. In NLP, modifying your own behaviour can make others change.

Voicing your thoughts and talking your way to success

Do you pay enough attention to what you say and how you say it? Do you know how much power and influence you have when you open your mouth? Tone, inflection, volume and pitch are all important areas to consider. Most people underestimate the significance of developing their speaking voice. Used correctly it is so persuasive but many people ignore this and rarely understand how to use it effectively. In NLP, people with the greatest choice and flexibility of behaviour come out on top. You have a voice, a great gift – don't waste your talent, make it work for you.

The easiest way to understand the adaptability of your voice is to compare it to a piece of music. Voice is the instrument of interpretation of the spoken word. Communication is a two-way process and if you are easy to listen to, those hearing you are likely to respond to you in a positive way. Those who have had some training in public speaking sometimes use mnemonics as memory joggers for optimum vocal effect. One simple example is R S V P P P: Rhythm, Speed, Volume, Pitch, Pause and Projection.

Rhythm is important because when you speak without variety of tone, you can anaesthetize your listener. By raising and lowering the voice to bring vocal sound to life you will keep your audience awake. Rhythm is directly linked to speed.

Speed variation is connected to the vocal rhythm. Varying speed makes for interested listeners and helps them maintain concentration. If you were, for example, recounting a story, speed helps to add excitement to the tale. But the speed of delivery should be matched with the volume you're speaking at.

Volume is something that obviously depends on where the conversation is taking place. It would be inappropriate to use loud volume when speaking in a one-to-one situation. However you'd probably need to increase it if you were talking in a crowded venue, such as a business reception or noisy work area. Volume is used mainly for emphasis and to command attention. Lowering your voice can add authority when telling an interesting story or giving advice.

Pitching the voice is something experienced public speakers do. They are trained to 'throw' their voice so that they can deliver their speech clearly to the audience in whatever size or shape of room they are speaking in. In general, it's irritating for any listener if they have to strain to hear what the speaker is saying. Correct use of mouth, jaw and lip muscles will produce properly accentuated words and assist with clear enunciation. You may find exercising your facial muscles and breathing a little deeper will ensure a variety of tone.

Pausing for effect is something worth practising. It can be the most effective use of your voice, though it is often ignored. A pause should last about four seconds. It might seem like an eternity, but anything shorter will go unnoticed by your listener. You can use the time to maintain good eye contact. Don't

> A pause should last about four seconds

forget the 'er' count. Filling spaces in conversation with props such as 'ers', 'ums' or 'you knows' where there should be pauses are clear signs of nervousness.

Finally, projection. This encompasses everything about the way you come across: power, personality, weight, authority, and expertise – what some people call 'clout'. If you want to persuade people to your way of thinking, or come across as an influential person, it pays to have some gravitas in your dealings with people. Projection is an art which can be practised. Remember to pay attention to experienced communicators – you can learn so much from watching them. Use those mirroring and modelling techniques which NLP practitioners know work well.

If possible, ask a friend or colleague to give you feedback on your voice and mannerisms. Unless you get an accurate appraisal, you could be wasting your opportunities for building rapport or creating impact. With practice you'll be surprised at how quickly some new habits can be adopted. Once you've started to develop some of the skills suggested here, the improvement in your vocal range and style of conversation will be much greater when you meet new people.

One important point to remember, and something that is referred to elsewhere in the book, is that you have two ears and one mouth, so use them in that proportion. It is good to be able to talk and use

> spend twice as much time listening as you do talking

your voice appropriately, but if you are able to spend twice as much time listening as you do talking, you will be creating a positive impression. People will regard you as a skilled communicator who knows how to initiate a conversation without dominating it.

Personal strengths and how to use them

People who know how to create the right impact are often capable of exerting a fair amount of influence. They are memorable for the right reasons. Every situation requires a slightly different focus. NLP states that people have all the resources they need; it is just a question of applying them.

Clothes and accessories are an important part of body language. In a business context what you wear should be conservative rather than fashionable and show authority or confidence. It's as well to express approachability too. If you know what image you want to create, be clear, not fussy. The aim is to build rapport and to be remembered positively. An outfit that fits well, is comfortable as well as being attractive and flattering, is ideal.

An easy way to outshine everyone and appear charming is to smile. Many people have wonderful natural smiles, but due to nervousness or apprehension, they are rarely seen. Sometimes all you can remember of someone is that their faces were set, the only thing registering were the stress muscles. A smile lights up a face – so use yours to good effect. People who smile easily give the impression of being pleasant, attractive, sincere and confident.

> People who smile easily give the impression of being pleasant, attractive, sincere and confident

It relaxes those with whom you are making contact. It also reassures other people when you are building rapport. It displays a positive attitude and openness in regard to giving and receiving feedback.

Establishing rapport is the biggest single determinant of successful communication and is inherent in NLP principles and basic techniques. All of the foregoing relates specifically to how to use your body and the language it speaks to best advantage.

Chapter 05
How your nervous system prepares you for anything

The nervous system's main role is to prepare your body either for action or for rest. It can be triggered involuntarily or as a deliberate response to a situation with which you are faced. Confronted with danger it will prepare you for 'fight or flight'. In relaxing or maybe boring circumstances, it will prepare you for rest or sleep.

Whatever your nervous system prepares you for, it has been stimulated by your senses and then supplies all your organs with what they need to handle a specific response.

The sensors to which your nervous system reacts are your eyes, ears, skin, nose and tongue. It is easy to envisage the different consequences of an ugly or beautiful sight, a harsh or harmonious sound, a revolting or delightful sensation, a nasty or pleasant smell, and a foul or delicious taste. Already you can appreciate that there is a vast range of sensations and their permutations to which your body and mind can react.

The organs and parts affected by your nervous system include your heart, lungs, muscles, digestive system, pupils, skin, sexual receptors and sphincter. Your balance and hearing can also be affected.

In 'fight or flight' mode your pupils will dilate, your heartbeat and blood pressure will increase, lungs will expand, muscles will be supplied with more blood, your digestive processes will slow down and your sphincter muscle will close. When preparing for repose, your pupils will become smaller, your heartbeat, blood pressure and lung volume will decrease, digestion will be easier and, last but not least, your sphincter will become relaxed.

CASE STUDY

The Russian scientist Ivan Pavlov is famously associated with 'Pavlov's dogs', an experiment in which dogs were deliberately conditioned to associate different stimuli with the presence of meat. In what may be an apocryphal story, a bell was rung every time that a dog was given meat. Because of the association of the bell with meat, the dog would therefore involuntarily salivate on each occasion the bell was rung, regardless of whether there was meat present or not. Its nervous system had therefore been subject to an unconscious learning process.

This demonstrates that the nervous system is not completely 'hardwired' and can be modified, through learning and recall, in its response to different stimuli. It is also the case that the body will shut down when subjected to extreme pain and stress, but whereas pain is a specifically induced sensation, stress can often be the product of a conditioned, or learned, response.

Hypnotism, a powerful tool for positive and negative effect

We are all aware of the effects of hypnotism and other forms of therapeutic activity and, of course, the conditioning process can also extend to brainwashing and the sometimes contradictory behaviour that often affects people when subject to the pressure of belonging to reactionary groups, whether political or religious.

Learning by association can be a powerful tool for good and fits well with NLP principles that seek to influence and persuade. The nervous system can thus be manipulated to respond positively in different situations but also needs to be consciously managed to avoid negative behaviours.

NLP recognizes different physical states in people and the many different signals they convey to those who have the necessary sensory perception to understand their meaning. Studying NLP principles provides a powerful insight into the effects of the nervous system as it integrates all the functions of mind and body.

This endorses the belief that 'people are not their behaviour' and the need, therefore, to practise the unconditional regard that will lead you to a better understanding of who they really are and why their patterns of speech and behaviour work as they do.

Technical aspects of the nervous system

There are two main parts of the nervous system, the central nervous system and the peripheral nervous system. The former consists of the brain and the spinal cord, while the latter is much more diffuse with 12 pairs of cranial nerves and 31 pairs of spinal nerves.

The central nervous system forms and stores memories, thoughts and emotions that are then connected to the muscles and glands through the peripheral nervous system.

The peripheral nervous system carries impulses to both sensory and motor nerves and manages the two-way 'traffic' with the central nervous system, which then decides, or not, to take action. The instantaneous response is either involuntary or has been preconditioned.

The so-called autonomic nervous system includes both central and peripheral nervous systems as involuntary controllers of heart muscle, smooth muscle and glands.

The 'fight or flight' response is regulated by the 'sympathetic' system that originates just in the spinal chord. The opposite (relaxing) response is regulated by the 'parasympathetic' system that originates from both brain and spinal cord (Table 5.1).

TABLE 5.1 Different roles for different systems

Sympathetic	Parasympathetic
Increases heart rate	Decreases heart rate
Increases blood glucose	Dilates visceral blood vessels
Diverts blood to skeletal muscle	Increases digestive activity
Activates body to deal with stress	Calms body – allows it to relax

Among others, the nerves affect the functions of:

- eyes – both movement and tears;
- tongue – and its various taste zones;
- larynx;
- lungs;
- heart;
- liver;
- bile duct;
- spleen;
- adrenal gland;
- kidney;
- stomach;
- bladder;
- prostate;
- bowel;
- uterus and testes.

The way the nervous system operates is like a shuttle service, with impulses racing to and from the brain to produce the appropriate physical and emotional reaction.

Your nervous system forces many different responses

Most people are nervous at the prospect of visiting the dentist and often a little tense when sitting in the dentist's chair. The anticipatory perception of drills, pliers, probes and white coats adds to the patient's apprehension. This is why dentists nowadays use soothing distractions such as music, television programmes showing above the chair, and hopefully, some sensitive rapport building before and during the treatment. The aim is to divert a sympathetic nervous system response to a parasympathetic nervous system response that induces well-being and relaxation. The dentist's verbal choice and body language also play an important part in the process and can make the difference between what could be a calm or terrifying prospect.

Whilst using dentistry as an illustration we can also take account of the role that local anaesthetics play in conjunction with the nervous system. The role of a local anaesthetic is to stop the impulses picked up by the sensory nerves and prevent them from passing to the central nervous system. As a result, we do not experience a sense of pain in the dental nerves.

In an organizational context, one of the most feared of activities is to give presentations. Research has shown that some people have an even greater fear of presentations than of death! The adrenaline stimulated by the prospect of standing up in front of an audience can either provoke better performance or it can result in poor performance.

Memories of past successes will work in favour of good performance, while memories of poor performance may act as a self-fulfilling prophecy. Fortunately, this shows that all people are susceptible to conditioning and therefore capable of improving their performance. It is a matter of determination, belief and learning the good habits of accomplished speakers that will result in success.

When speaking in front of others, the nervous system heightens awareness and stimulates the faculties to the extent that presenters often speak too quickly for their audiences. This is one reason why trainers in presentation skills often advise their students to deliberately speak at half their normal pace. This usually results in a delivery that seems to the presenter to be very slow, but is in reality the pace at which he or she usually speaks anyway.

When a speaker is in presenting mode, the increased stimulation of the senses means that much more information than usual will be simultaneously absorbed through eyes and ears. This can sometimes give a surreal effect akin to being an outside observer in a trance-like state. Far from being a threat to the presentation, it equips speakers to be more effective in thinking on their feet.

Audiences and their responses will also influence the effectiveness of a speech. The worldwide public speaking network Toastmasters insists that everyone who presents to one of their meetings is greeted warmly, applauded at the beginning and applauded at the end of the speech. This is to reinforce their feeling of being supported and appreciated for what they are doing and is intended to create a platform for better performance. The speakers' sensory receptors encourage a feeling of (relative) confidence that is then reflected in the capabilities that they are consequently able to display. Arguably, this is something that politicians, in particular, would die for.

Speaking in front of friends is one thing. Speaking to a hostile audience is quite another. There is no better example than in Mark Anthony's speech to the Romans following Julius Caesar's murder in Shakespeare's play of the same name. 'Friends, Romans, countrymen, lend me your ears. I come to bury Caesar not to praise him' are words designed to neutralize a hostile reaction prior to sticking the metaphorical dagger into Brutus as an 'honourable man'. The repetition of that phrase, and a progressively increasing sense of irony, was designed ultimately to destroy Brutus's credibility and reverse the mood of the crowd. This was, in effect, a conditioning process to overcome an otherwise spontaneous negative response.

If you understand the role of the nervous system, NLP believes that you will have a greater ability to use it to your advantage.

Chapter 06
The incredible power of language

Language is wonderfully fluid, dynamic and surprising. It can induce laughter, tears, anger, doubt and pride, create a feeling of calm, incite action – even to the extent of rebellion and war – and invoke many other responses and emotions.

Language can also be used to clarify and obscure truth. It can encourage positive outcomes for both parties to a piece of communication or it can be used to manipulate the outcome in one party's favour. Understanding the role and effect of language enables NLP to be applied as a powerful influence on the outcomes you want.

If you were to ask the question of a colleague 'How well is it going?', the reply is most likely to be along the lines of 'Quite well, thanks', or 'Could be better, I suppose.' The generalized question produces a generalized answer and very little information will have been transmitted or received.

If you asked the question 'Have you finished the report you were writing?', this is a specific question that invites the specific answer 'Yes' or 'No'. If you want specific information, you have to ask specific questions. There is nothing wrong with generalizations in the right context but they are more likely to set a mood than to result in a specific outcome.

NLP's purpose for language is that it will be used for the good of individuals and organizations, serve a therapeutic as well as a motivational purpose and help personal understanding, learning and development.

Language is about how we interact with the world and includes the process of filtering the meaning of words and phrases according to our own personal experiences and preconditioning. There are dozens of ways in which we do this and this chapter contains illustrations of the main filters we employ. In the same way that a camera has short, medium and long focus that can include or exclude or blur elements of the picture, so we all have our own set of lenses, and they are different from everyone else's. What pleases one person can totally displease another. Ironically, when we use vague language, we still expect others to understand us perfectly, yet often become impatient if they do not express themselves clearly.

> What pleases one person can totally displease another

We also have to deal with negative as well as positive inclinations both when we speak and when we receive information from others. The negative is summarized by what we don't want and the positive is summarized by what we do want. That song by an arguing couple whose words begin 'Anything you can do I can do better, I can do anything better than you' includes a series of 'Yes I can', 'No, you can't', 'Yes I can', 'No you can't' as each of the singers claims to be superior. This neatly encapsulates positive and negative frames of mind we constantly face.

In simple terms, language has a number of dos and don'ts that are relatively easy to remember and apply. By thinking of real-life situations with which we are familiar, you can then easily attach them to particular principles.

Why are you so boring?

As one well-known actor is supposed to have said to another, 'Well, that's enough about you. Let's talk about me.' If you ask yourself why you find some people at parties so boring and then analyse the reason why, you will quickly observe that it is because their main focus is on themselves and their interests and not on you. By comparison, if you ask why others can be so interesting, it is because what they talk about will be centred on you and topics that might fascinate and surprise you. Rapport, as an important building block of NLP, depends on being audience-centred and finding common ground on which to converse.

A good rule of thumb in any kind of exercise that is intended to engage an audience is to apply the 'two to one' ratio. That is to say you should use the words you, your and yours twice as much as I, me and mine. In a marketing context, if you continually go on about 'us' as an organization, our superb products and first-class service, that will have less impact than talking about what 'you' can achieve with them. Writing about yourself comes last and not first. If, as an experiment, you were to check out a few commercial websites and count how many times they refer to 'our company, its policies, mission and achievements' compared to what specifically their customers would achieve, you would be likely to find that those that are audience-focused are harder to find than those that are quite obviously self-absorbed.

Why do I find it difficult to understand what you say or write?

There are many reasons why you could be difficult to understand. They could include speech that is inaudible, too fast a pace of delivery, too many topics covered at once or a failure to recognize the likely rate and process by which listener and reader absorb information.

A further factor could be the lengths of the sentences that you use. Research on sentence lengths and their likely effectiveness in creating an impact shows that the shorter the sentence length, the greater impact it will achieve. This can be seen to good effect in popular newspapers where average sentence length is fairly short at around 8–12 words to a sentence, compared to the so-called quality publications where it will generally be more than 20. There is a good reason for this, in that popular papers are as much about entertaining their readers as informing them. The quality papers have readers who are consumers more of information than entertainment. Because of their willingness to absorb information, readers will happily make the effort to digest more sophisticated communication about more complex ideas, comment and argument.

Put another way, readers for example of the United Kingdom's *Sun* newspaper are likely to want quick, compelling and easily accessible stories than the ostensibly boring detail of say, complex economic performance data. 'Freddie Starr ate my hamster' was a *Sun* headline that had immediate impact and is still remembered today, whereas 'Social trends in shrinking mining communities' will be long forgotten. The first is sheer drama, while the second, we might suppose, just attracts cerebral interest.

Why is it easier to recall some uses of language than others?

Journalists, as professional writers who must 'sell' their stories, are fully aware of the need, first of all, to attract the reader's attention and interest. In fact, it is sub-editors rather than the journalists themselves who usually write the headlines, but based on the likely attractiveness of the story itself. The criterion for a good news story is often explained as 'Dog bites man' is not newsworthy but 'Man bites dog' is. There needs to be an 'angle' that causes people to sit up and take notice because it causes a stress or tension in the mind that is out of the ordinary. 'Freddie Starr ate my hamster' is a rather exceptional example of this but nonetheless a valid illustration.

There are many examples of the way language is used to make an impact. If you think of the famous quotations that you recall, there is usually a device or a stress that is used so that your mind immediately records a 'difference'. In the late President John Kennedy's address to an audience in Germany when he announced 'Ich bin ein Berliner', it was the incongruity of an American speaking in German, despite the fact that he was known not to speak German, that created the twist. The fact that 'ein Berliner', unbeknown to him, was the name of a doughnut, has made it even more memorable for some.

Sir Winston Churchill famously said of Clement Attlee, his opposite number in the UK Labour Party that he was 'A modest little man... with much to be modest about' – a seeming compliment twisted to become a stinging insult.

A similar twist is attributed to Groucho Marx, who said that he would not want to belong to a club that would accept him as a member – still memorable after half a century.

Poetry uses such devices as repeated use of single consonants or vowels (alliteration) to create a particular effect. In Alfred Noyes' 'The Highwayman' the eponymous horseman's echoing, noisy arrival at the inn is audibly portrayed by the words 'Over the cobbles he clattered and clashed in the dark inn-yard', where 'cobbles', 'clattered' and 'clashed' are hard-sounding words that emulate the imagined sound of a horse's hooves.

In a different context, people often recall, for a very long time, sentences about them that begin with 'you'. If someone says, 'You are very wise to say that' or 'You are the best person I've ever had doing that job', the chances are that you will remember for a long time what was said and the circumstances in which it was said. Similarly, if someone says to you 'You'll never be as good as him', or 'You have disappointed me', these statements will remain etched on your mind.

There are, of course, other factors at play besides the word 'you' in such sentences, as they go to the heart of your feelings about yourself. Such is our sensitivity about ourselves that 'you' sentences are able to penetrate more deeply than talk about, for example, ideas, activities and other people.

Is spelling really that important?

It is, of course, important that we are able to apply some consistent standards to the tools we use for communication so that we can pin down a code by which any variations to that standard may be judged. The alternative is a progressive dissipation of the code and an even harder job to understand the different variants as they evolve. There are already some notable trends in the evolution of language as it applies to e-mails, texts and other electronic communication. If there were no standards for spelling, the language could get out of hand.

However, in terms of understanding words, literal spelling may not be as important as it seems. The text below has been widely circulated in the press and on the internet and illustrates that there are other factors at play when reading the written word. This has to do with our brains and the fact that they create a kind of shorthand so that we can absorb information more quickly and easily than if reading every word in its entirety.

If you can read the previous paragraph and understand it, you will be able to understand the self-explanatory passage below. NLP recognizes the minimization process that takes place when acquiring the habit of communicating more efficiently.

cdnuolt blveiee taht I cluod aulaclty uesdnatnrd
waht I was rdanieg. The
phaonmneal pweor of the hmuan mnid. Aoccdrnig to a
rscheearch taem at
Cmabrigde Uinervtisy, it deosn't mttaer in waht
oredr the ltteers in a
wrod are, the olny iprmoatnt tihng is taht the
frist and lsat ltteer be
in the rghit pclae. The rset can be a taotl mses
and you can sitll raed
it wouthit a porbelm. Tihs is bcuseae the huamn
mnid deos not raed ervey
lteter by istlef, but the wrod as a wlohe. Amzanig
huh? yaeh and I
awlyas tghuhot slpeling was ipmorantt!

Why do some people overload my brain?

When people want to impress, they sometimes use a torrent of words that mimic 'business speak' but deny any coherent meaning.

Many politicians could be legitimately accused of obscuring meaning with fine-sounding phrases just so that they sound impressive. The passage below is from one such European politician and your challenge would be to work out what he is actually saying.

Some years ago, the European Commission set up a 'fight the fog' campaign to reduce the growing amount of jargon creeping into everyday use within the European Union's administration. In the case below, the campaign seems not to have been very successful:

> The reform strategy proposals identify the ways to efficiently integrate assessment of resources with decisions on positive and crucially negative priorities. A system of activity-based management will be introduced, facilitated by strategic planning and programming arrangements...

There are two basic steps to understanding what people are saying. The first is to decode the language and the second is to understand the meaning. If the language contains too many different elements, then understanding will be made much more difficult. If we take the phrase 'efficiently integrate assessment of resources' from the above, we have to consider four separate elements in the space of just five words. By the time you think about efficiency, integration, assessment and resources all being compacted into what is intended to be a single meaning, you may well have lost any thread of meaning intended by the sentence.

An important tenet of NLP is movement towards a clearly defined outcome. If you can sense the direction that a sentence is taking, your brain will automatically fill in the meaning – much in the same way as if you are given the first and last letters of a word, as in the previous section, but the rest of the letters are in a jumble, you will know what that word is.

In the politician's passage above, we are given no real clues about the direction we are going in, nor what, in specific terms, it is really about. NLP would say that if we knew the context, we might have some chance of deciphering the message. However, it is still far too wordy to be clear.

The curse of generalization

'I don't think you are ready for promotion just yet' must be one of the more soul-destroying things you can say to an ambitious and capable employee. Without any evidence criteria, it is a generalization that means nothing but at the same time has a negative effect.

CASE STUDY

The managing director of a prominent household furniture company decided that in order to increase management effectiveness within the business, the best young talent should be selected from within it and put on an 18-month management development programme. The company would then be able to recruit competent, well-trained people more readily from within as compared to seeking external candidates with all the cost and risk associated with that process.

However, because the company's regional management had not fully bought in to the managing director's project, and despite new, well-trained talent now being available, they continued to select mostly from external candidates. In justifying it to those who had been trained, several of them said that they didn't think they were yet ready for a management position. The outcome has been a lot of money spent on expensive training but has created six or so disaffected individuals now well placed and active in looking for better jobs outside the company.

This has been almost entirely due to a common management practice of using generalizations in order to avoid detail or any logical argument. It is frequently used to keep people in their place.

If there had been a specific reason given, or a conditional next step indicated on the route towards promotion, the trainee managers would have understood a route forward and probably cooperated. As it is, the company's competitors now have access to good young managers that someone else has paid to train.

Although generalizations can be a powerful tool for the good in certain circumstances, they are frequently used to exert power and control over others. This is because you cannot easily argue against a generalization since it is mainly opinion and not fact based.

'People are not going to like that' is an assertion that means nothing unless you know how many, why, and any other factual basis for the statement. So, too, if you said to someone that 'You are so obviously wrong', there is nothing to show that it is either obvious or that the person is wrong.

Similarly, there is no point in saying 'It's because I know I'm right' unless there is concrete and factual evidence that you can use to support that position. 'I only argue when I know I'm right' is a clever twist on this manipulative ploy. The only fact in the situation is that you believe it, not that it is right.

UK Prime Minister Tony Blair famously justified invading Iraq by saying: 'It's because I really believe that it's the right thing to do', thus saving himself the problem of explaining the reason on evidence-based terms – a huge generalization that has had profound international consequences.

NLP enables you to train yourself to recognize the difference in validity of different words and phrases and therefore to be more confident in expressing contrary arguments.

The benefits of generalization

Generalization can create efficiency in the learning process. At its most basic level, a child that has been stung by stinging nettles learns that, generally speaking, plants can cause an unpleasant sensation and so he or she becomes cautious when walking in wooded areas. The generalization process has extended the stinging experience into a wider context. When you learn to drive, you do not just learn to drive down the roads of which you have had previous experience. You know you are capable of driving down any road.

Generalization can stimulate emotion because behind a phrase or sentence is a wealth of meaning based on previous knowledge and experience. When Sir Winston Churchill declaimed about fighting the enemy 'whatever the cost may be, we shall fight them on the beaches, we shall fight on the landing grounds, we shall fight in the fields and in the streets, we shall fight in the hills; we shall never surrender…', although the different elements of the speech sound specific, they are in fact generalizations. Our response to 'fight', or 'fight them on the beaches' is to elaborate in our minds and fill in the gaps as we visualize what it means to fight and then imagine the scene on the beach – the men, the ships, the military equipment, the sea defences and so on.

A further example of generalization concerns the use of indirect as compared to direct language. 'It was decided to open the new sports hall in October' leaves hanging who it was that made the decision. If it was an individual, the project team, the committee or the local council, it would be more direct and informative to say, for example, 'The committee decided to open the new sports hall in October'.

Generalization can give us a set of rules that enable us to filter and respond to different circumstances in the way that best suits our personal view of the world.

The use of language to distort the truth

If your words have ever been distorted and used against you, you will know how completely frustrating that feels. Similarly, there are situations in the workplace where you may feel that people or situations have been misrepresented.

A good example of this could be the way a meeting you attended has been reported. Those who chair meetings or who write the minutes of a meeting have a very tempting opportunity to report matters as they see them so that it is their point of view that prevails. The language used in minutes can very much colour the impact they create.

As the following three illustrations demonstrate, when writing minutes, you have options as to the way you express things. The first is verbatim reporting that just records a conversation but shows that differences exist between two people and that a third is probably impatient. In fact, it goes nowhere:

Jean expressed concern to John that his staff members were under-performing. John said that, in his view, this was not the case and Jean was welcome to have a look at the most recent appraisal records. Max suggested that Jean and John sort out the difference of view between them and we should all move onto a new subject.

The second is more direct and succinct and leads to an outcome.

Staff performance issues: John and Jean to agree if any action is required and report to the next meeting.

The third uses loaded language to imply a real problem and a management deficiency:

The performance of John's staff was giving cause for concern, although John was apparently not aware of this.

The use of the word 'apparently' can be used in its literal, neutral sense or it can be used destructively as in the above sentence. It is also likely that different people will read it in different ways.

In a positive way, you can use distortion of the truth to suit a particular situation. If you watch Walt Disney's cartoons, you convert animated drawings into believable situations and very much get involved in the story. Why else would you feel emotion at, for example, the death of Bambi's mother? It's only a drawing but we have made it real. The same applies to the things we read and the things we hear.

It is a central mechanism in NLP that in order to create change in ourselves and others, we can creatively imagine what that change looks, sounds and feels like.

Why can I not remember the names of people that I have just been introduced to?

When you meet a group of people for the first time and the host goes round the room introducing you to the different individuals, you are only too aware that you will have difficulty remembering some of their names later. This is in part due to the many different things that are already going on in your mind and

> the mind deletes some information in favour of other messages

partly to do with the fact that the mind deletes some information in favour of other messages that you will be consciously or unconsciously receiving.

This is a well-known phenomenon that Noam Chomsky introduced in a mid-1950s thesis as being psychological filters that people use to modify information that they receive. In this particular case, information that cannot be managed efficiently is 'deleted' from the mind.

Research suggests that our minds can only handle around seven pieces of information in any one 'bundle'. The number may be slightly higher on a good day or slightly lower on a bad one. This is why those who are trained to give presentations, write reports or teach are advised to limit lists of points to just seven. Your local telephone number is unlikely to contain more than seven digits and your regional code is separated out from it in order not to create an extended string of numbers that no one will remember. The archetypal picture of a prisoner serving his time is to scratch a vertical mark on his cell wall for each of six days and then strike the marks through with a diagonal line to denote that a full week has elapsed. Passing time is not represented by a continuous series of vertical scratch marks. We need the bundling mechanism in order to give us the picture that will be easiest to assimilate.

Why can 'should', 'ought' and other words and phrases be so irritating?

For some reason, people do not like being told what they ought to do, but probably don't know how to explain why they don't like it. 'Should' and 'ought' often masquerade as positive words when the underlying sentiment behind them, intentionally or not, is to position the speaker as better informed and the listener less so.

'You should get that seen to' may be irritating because the listener already knows it. 'You ought to know better' positions the speaker in a parental mode against which the listener may potentially react.

However, the words can be received positively if expressed in the form of a neutral question such as, 'What do you think you should do about it?' which gives the status back to the listener (assuming tone and body language were already neutral). This enables the person being questioned to provide his or her own answer or to say 'I'm not really sure. What would you do?' Because the speaker has now been given 'permission' to express an opinion, it can no longer give any offence.

Using 'should' and 'ought' is to generalize, as it provides no detail or evidence as to why. If you started off with the evidence, it would be easier to plant the idea.

In addition to 'ought' and 'should' are other words and phrases that more directly convey negative and often demotivating meaning. These include 'shouldn't', 'won't', 'don't', 'can't', 'mustn't', 'never', 'needless', 'unnecessary' and many more.

The passage below is from a real memo sent to staff in a real organization just a year or so ago. It has only been modified so as not to identify the organization in question. Ten of the staff were questioned about the memo and their feelings about it, and all of them felt that it was negatively expressed even though its purpose was a good one.

SECURITY POLICY

We have had various incidents recently where our security has been breached. Some have had the potential to lead to serious accidents and one resulted in a theft.

We have a duty of care to everyone who works in the building and anyone who uses the building. It has therefore become necessary to ask everyone to review their working practices.

I have listed some guidelines below:

If you use keys on a daily basis, and do not take them home, have they been returned to a secure location, ie Security Office, at the end of the day?

If you are responsible for locking and unlocking fire exits please make sure that they are unlocked if people are in the building – or use appropriate signage to direct people to alternate safe exits.

NEVER prop a pass door open.

NEVER leave the workshop/testing area doors open when there are no visitors unless you are working in that area.

All guests/visitors *MUST* be signed in at Reception.

ALWAYS use lockers provided or lock your belongings in your office.

Do *NOT* go onto the factory floor unless you have permission from a workshop technician.

Do not enter the workshop unless you have permission (Henry can be contacted via tannoy).

ALWAYS CHECK that a door has closed and locked itself behind you where security is vulnerable.

NB: It is the responsibility of every member of staff to keep the Business Premises safe and secure. Any breaches of Security will be viewed seriously.

Bold capitals are a form of shouting and to some degree will insult the intelligence of the reader. The writer mixes imperative words like 'never', 'must' and 'always' with indirect language such as 'It has therefore become necessary to ask' and 'will be viewed seriously' rather than 'I ask' or 'I will view seriously'. This is a mismatch to the otherwise direct style of the memo. There is nothing about it that implies any rapport.

Why are some people so easy and some so difficult to converse with?

People differ widely in their orientation that can be influenced by values, culture, physiology, experiences and preferences.

In a work context, there are people whose predominant style variously orientates them to tasks, processes, technologies, creativity, control, influence, passivity or other characteristics. Their response to communication is substantially governed by these personal orientations.

There are also those who when faced with a particular communication will either be looking for something that stands out as being an exception or they will be looking for conformity to the rule.

In addition, there are those who seek new ideas and challenges and those firmly anchored in the 'now' – the creators as compared to the repairers.

The US firm Thomas International offers a psychometric test that evaluates someone's personality on the basis of comparative Dominance, Influence, Steadiness and Compliance (DISC) and matches personal profiles to job suitability. Leadership, marketing and selling roles usually suit people with higher scores in dominance and influence, whereas, for example, with a computer programmer you would tend to look for steadiness and compliance as essential personality traits.

Although the human race shares so much in common, even marginal differences in personality, values and beliefs make a profound difference to the way individuals handle information, and it is these differences that NLP highlights.

What is the solution to others' imprecise communication?

The strongest tool at our disposal is the ability to ask questions. If someone says 'George doesn't like frivolity at work', you can only guess what is meant by frivolity. It may be that he doesn't like laughter or jokes or horseplay or just happy conversation, but you don't know until you have asked a question about what he means by frivolity. Also, you do not know whether it was a single circumstance that prompted George to make a comment about frivolity or whether that is his general position. Neither do you know whether such a remark, even if indeed he made one, was directed at a single individual or at employees in general.

As mentioned previously, if told 'You are not yet ready for promotion', it means nothing unless you can ask precisely what is meant by that statement. You will want to know the specific skills, knowledge and experience that are perceived to be lacking, what you must do to demonstrate 'readiness' and when, and under what circumstances, you can expect a promotion.

Rudyard Kipling summarizes questioning techniques best in his well-known poem:

I keep six faithful serving men
Who teach me well and true
Their names are *what* and *where* and *when*
And *how* and *why* and *who*

This poem is also extremely useful when putting together a piece of communication yourself and a well-practised technique for curing 'writers block'.

Why do I recall some brand names and not others?

Organizations can spend a huge amount of time and money agonizing over their names. Some employ agencies to do it, while others endeavour to go it alone.

If you see a particular brand name every day, such as Esso, Marks & Spencer, Ford or even HM Revenue & Customs, then there is no difficulty whatsoever in recognizing it and broadly what it stands for. If you come across a brand less frequently, it is important that there is something about it that also makes it easier to recall.

CASE STUDY

A Gloucestershire company that specializes in marketing services used to use three different brand names for the different aspects of its service. These companies were called Business Marketing Analysis, Business Data Sales and Business to Business Direct. The shorthand version of these companies was The Business Group.

Research into clients' perception and recall of these brand names demonstrated clearly that, whereas the names of their contacts in these companies were easily remembered, the brand names were not. Only one client, Kraft Foods, could accurately recall a brand name correctly but also volunteered the comment 'I think they have a branding problem.'

As a consequence, the company decided to change its name and consolidate from three (or four) brand names to one but needed something to help it stand out from the crowd. A brainstorming session plus some timely serendipity produced the suggestion 'Blue Sheep'. Instead of the raised eyebrows that such a suggestion might normally cause, the immediate response was to accept it subject to 'sleeping on it overnight'. Blue Sheep is now universally recognized in its chosen market and has considerably accelerated its growth.

From a communications perspective the name fits in with NLP theory in that it is concrete and specific and not an abstract or general one that would be harder to recall. It is also incongruous and contradictory in that there is no such thing as a blue sheep. This 'twist' improves its memorability.

The designers commissioned to come up with a logo for the newly named company, initially submitted drawn illustrations of a blue sheep in various styles but realised that a greater impact would be created if a 'real' blue sheep could be photographed instead. Anyone can draw a blue sheep but it would be highly exceptional to find one that was actually blue. To this day we do not know whether the sheep was dyed blue or the photographic image was tinted blue!

As a general communications principle, it is easier to convey memorable meaning through tangible objects than abstract ideas. The model in Figure 6.1 may usefully be employed to benchmark any piece of communication that you want to make for impact or recall.

FIGURE 6.1 The two right-hand boxes hold the key to memorability

Abstract	Concrete
General	Specific

Recall demonstrates that a learning process has taken place. Learning processes work best when linking into what people already know or have experienced; something against which they can put a frame of reference. Abstraction and generality, by definition, have no perceptible framework to the reader or listener.

You can apply these principles to marketing, design, selling, appraising, instructing, presenting, informing, warning and many other communications uses.

Why could it be 'all Greek to me'?

More than 2,000 years ago, Aristotle wrote his *Poetics* to explain the essential components in Greek and Roman drama and poetry and to describe their effect on audiences. What he wrote is an essential part of the study of language and is still relevant today. To understand the *Poetics* is to understand the impact of language and situations, and is complementary to an appreciation of NLP.

There are many terms used in the description of Greek literature and the main ones, still in use in contemporary study, are as follows:

- *Catharsis* describes the effect of feeling purged and relieved after you have been through an emotional roller-coaster. It is used today by psychotherapists to bring out deep emotions that have never previously been expressed and provides a cleansing psychological effect.

- *Comic relief* is often used in serious situations to relieve tension and in drama, to highlight the tragic element in a situation. Laughter is a well-known stress-relief mechanism and helps people to cope.

- *Hubris* is often described as 'pride going before a fall' and is a characteristic of otherwise powerful and competent people who ignore warnings of failure because, in their view, they know best. This will inevitably lead to a fall.

- *Metaphor* is used by most of us to explain something in terms of something else; 'iron curtain', 'pink pound', 'vulture capitalists', 'glass ceiling' and 'mushroom management' are all examples.

- *Pathos*, from which the word 'pathetic' derives, is something that we see, read or hear that evokes feelings of tenderness, pity or sorrow.

- *Suspension of disbelief* is when, for example, you watch a play or a film and experience genuine emotions despite knowing that what you see is not real but an acted representation.

- *Euphemism* is the expression of something in agreeable terms to the listener or reader when it should more truthfully be harsh or unpleasant.

- *Irony*, a characteristic of British humour not always shared by other nationalities, is meaning one thing but saying another. The classic example from Shakespeare's *Julius Caesar* is 'For Brutus is an honourable man', with the inference that he is anything but.

NLP, as a modern creation, has been described as eclectic and owes much of its thinking to philosophers and psychologists over the centuries. Far from plagiarizing others' ideas, its strength is in the way it has gathered together powerful thinking and communication techniques and packaged the best of them so that they are available to everyone in a contemporary context.

Chapter 07
Rapport: your most important communications tool

The art of making personal contact

Many things in life start and end with good interaction with other people. That is why acquiring NLP skills is important. In the workplace this is particularly so because you need people to remember you favourably. If they do, it is because you are memorable and it is probably due to creating rapport.

Building relationships with others takes time, commitment and effort. You need to be focused, self-disciplined and have patience. If people like you, they will probably be happy to do what you want, it's as simple as that. In the workplace if you can develop the ability to build relationships with other people, you will be well ahead of the crowd. Rapport is about the creation of trust, inspiring confidence, displaying a positive attitude, being prepared to give (and take) feedback and the ability to mirror other people. This is one of the main NLP techniques.

Creating rapport is a really important skill. It could be defined as the ability to communicate meaningfully with someone based on mutual understanding, congruity and trust. It is promoted by matching behaviour at a conscious level to achieve complete and valuable communication with another person. There are NLP-related techniques which will help you towards good communication with individuals. They are easy to use and, when put into effect, have a dramatic ability to change the outcome of communication.

Can you recall recently listening to two people in conversation who used similar gestures, words and phrases? Was the tone of the conversation amicable and positive? Did they express similar views and use complementary body language? If so, this would indicate that these individuals enjoyed a high level of rapport.

Conversely when two people are using different language styles, words, tone of voice, gestures and behaviour, despite trying to relate successfully, they are likely to experience frustration and lack of understanding or agreement.

It is by using comparable posture, expression, breathing, movement, voice and language patterns when communicating (and this applies within reason whether in person, on the phone or in written language) that people stand the best chance of achieving a good level of mutual trust and persuasion.

When looking at building rapport, remember that it is not confined to communication between two people. Rapport is a means of influencing others and it is successfully used in many large companies to ensure cohesiveness throughout an organization. Enlightened managers who deal successfully with their staff will use a style which is not full of jargon, aggressive or inflexible. Those who have studied NLP will have an adaptable management style. This can effectively reduce division across the workplace and promote harmonious relationships among colleagues and staff. The higher the level of rapport you can create with people directly corresponds to the amount of influence you can exert on them.

One way to begin building rapport with someone is to note the mannerisms that the other uses. By 'matching' or 'mirroring' their posture, movement, voice or conversational style, the greater likelihood you'll have of developing a relaxed way of communicating with the people you encounter. It can be deliberate but often people find themselves doing it unconsciously.

In NLP one of the core beliefs is that mind and body are part of the same process, as in the section 'mind and body are inextricably linked' on page 19 (see also Chapter 3, The mind and its effects on your behaviour). Rapport is essential for any meaningful communication to occur: whether your desire is to persuade, engage someone's attention, or effectively chair a meeting.

So why build rapport with other people? There are many reasons. One is because it's practical, another that it aids communication, and also you can learn a great deal from others. Think of the most successful people you know, do they know how to build rapport? They probably do it extremely well. Interpersonal skills are not dependent on background, education or wealth. Anyone can do it – though people with the greatest choice and flexibility of behaviour come out on top.

The advantages of rapport building

- Recognition: creating impact when you meet people. You never get a second chance to make a first impression.

- Recall: if someone can recall you easily, you've come across well when you were first introduced.

- Reaction: one of the most desirable things is a positive reaction when you encounter someone again.

- Respect: aim to gain someone's trust. The ability to cooperate with and assist others is vital. You will earn respect if you can do this.

- Responsibility: you should take responsibility for building rapport with others. This will mean you are in control of your relationships, both professional and social. Don't allow others, or yourself, to mess it up.

Having the ability to build rapport is a powerful resource. You will learn to be flexible and adaptable as the same methods won't work every time with each person you meet. In NLP it states that success depends on varying what you do until you get the result that you want. Your objectives may change as you go along. But you can modify your behaviour to achieve your plans. Are you, for example, focusing on career, self-development, social or business success? To be successful at building rapport, you need to put other people first. They are the most important part. Developing interpersonal skills and creating trust is paramount. Remember that people are not their words and behaviour – you may have to suspend judgement when first meeting people if you are not naturally attuned to them.

Take, for example, rapport in the context of professional relationships. The advantage of building good rapport with colleagues is that you are going to be well (if not better) informed than others. This saves you valuable time and increases your ability to communicate. You also pick up on internal politics and are able to maximize opportunities that come your way. Externally you will develop valuable contacts who act as referrers, bridges, sources, links and influencers to help you achieve your personal goals.

Key skills in building rapport

The key skills required when building rapport with others are enquiring, listening, researching and organizing. Some recent success stories are given below.

CASE STUDY

A newly formed IT company wanted to find investors. They worked hard to develop relationships with a number of potential funders. First they spent six months researching suitable prospects, through influential people who gave them advice and suggested the way forward. Then they identified a number of venture capitalists and investors. From several introductions they found three companies who were prepared to help them. The IT company now has sufficient investment for their growth over the next five years. Their business is on track to perform to its maximum potential.

If they had not taken the time to build rapport with several different parties, their organization would have become unviable. This example shows that it can make all the difference between success and failure of a business enterprise. NLP states that people will normally make the best choice available to them in any given situation.

CASE STUDY

An international firm of consulting engineers wanted to improve their ability to win more business in the United Kingdom and Europe. Their business development strategy was to involve all their staff in increasing their links with the most relevant movers and shakers in the construction and property industry. Everyone from the chairman down to the newest and most junior employee was encouraged to work hard to raise the company's profile within their profession. It is not only the high-flyers in an organization that are influential. They nurtured their contacts and built strong strategic alliances with a number of other firms. As a result they have recently won a number of internationally acclaimed projects as well as national and international awards. In NLP people have all the resources they need; it is just a question of applying them.

CASE STUDY

A high-profile UK architectural practice carried out a client satisfaction survey to benchmark their reputation. They compiled questionnaires, interviewed a selection of clients, prospects and influencers. The partners took a risk in commissioning the survey. After all they could have received a lot of adverse criticism. But they were prepared for this. Their attitude was that if the results were unfavourable, don't think 'failure', think 'opportunity to learn'. The results of the survey reflected the company's strengths and identified areas where improvements could be made. By following up on some of the encouraging comments received, the directors were able to acquire repeat business and new work which increased their annual turnover by almost 20 per cent. NLP belief states it is you who has control of your mind and therefore the results that you achieve.

CASE STUDY

A charity had to organize a high-profile fundraiser at a time when there were a number of other similar events. Apathy had set in, take-up on table bookings were slow and ticket sales were sluggish. The organizers took stock of the situation and decided that, rather than cancel the event, they needed to harness energy and support from their staff to take the project forward. By calling in favours from some of the charity's high-profile patrons and supporters, it was possible to rekindle enthusiasm and energize volunteers. A brainstorming session took place among a group of individuals who had diverse skills and personality types. A number of new initiatives were suggested. Everyone took on a role that played to their personal strengths. The result: the project went forward with eagerness because volunteers worked harmoniously and productively together. The event was a sell-out. NLP states that modifying your own behaviour can make others change.

> Most people work best with people they know and trust

All the above examples show, in a business context, the value of building rapport with other people. Most people work best with people they know and trust. To be successful at building rapport requires the development of a genuine interest in other people. Here is a mnemonic to help you:

R A P P O R T: Relationships are powerful providing opportunities and rewards today.

Relationship building skills are of great value, because if you can acquire them you will be more successful than people who don't have them. This involves getting to know people and valuing their friendship. Rapport building is like a treasure hunt. You don't know who you are going to meet or what you may find out. But you can get amazing results. You will need to adopt new habits and move outside your comfort zone to develop rapport with different types of people. Utilizing NLP skills will unleash the power available to you and will help you achieve far more than you expected.

Be curious: making new friends

You'll find it easier to build rapport with people if you can manage a bit of 'small talk'. If you are building rapport for business or professional reasons, it's important to get off on the right foot. One way is to ask appropriate questions. Be curious – because it is far more important to be interested in others, than to be interesting yourself.

Perhaps you should start by reviewing your networking skills to see if they are effective and up to date:

- Do you communicate regularly only with people you know well?

- Do you seek to increase or refresh your circle of acquaintances, make new friends, get to know new colleagues?

- Do you prefer formal introductions or are you happier operating in an informal way?

- Do you ever ask your friends or colleagues to introduce you to new people?

Depending on the answers to the above questions, it might be worth looking at some ways to refresh your rapport-building skills:

- Get organized: preparation is essential. Rapport building isn't everyone's strongest suit.

- Have a plan. If you don't know why you're doing something, you won't do it well.

- If you're apprehensive about trying new things, a bit of preparation will make you less wary.

- Be decisive. Dithering gets you nowhere.

- Be positive and outwardly confident when meeting new people.

- For impact work on your opening lines.

- Good posture is important, stand up straight when being introduced to new people.

- Maintain appropriate eye contact (there is more about this in the chapter on 'The body and its impact on communication').

- Finally, try to relax. If you can't relax, take some deep breaths. At least then you'll be able to speak.

Rapport is a two-way thing, so try not to dominate any exchange you are taking part in. (This is something to remember if due to nerves you tend to talk too much.) Once you have finished 'transmitting' make sure you switch to 'receive' mode to allow the other person to speak. If you are being monopolized by a bore with a loud voice on an uninteresting topic, you'll want to make a discreet exit. Get ready to make a graceful withdrawal and make your excuse politely but firmly. Say something like 'I'm sorry, but I see my colleague is about to leave and I need to speak to him.'

One of the skills of having good rapport is being memorable. Politeness and courtesy will make you unforgettable. People who are always charming are hard to dislike. Dealing with people appropriately, kindly and sympathetically is one way to start. Take pride in what you do and be professional. Whatever the occasion, you don't know who you will meet or who will see you there. When conversing with others keep your tone friendly; people are more likely to want to talk to you if you do this.

Building rapport with people you work with is an important skill in business. Technical skills are no longer enough on their own; relationships and the ability to influence others help you build networks that everyone needs to succeed. After all, people tend to like people who remind them of themselves.

Creating an atmosphere of understanding and respect, as well as the ability to follow and accept someone else's point of view (even if it is different from your own) is what you are aiming for. This is often referred to as 'being on the same wavelength'. Where you want to make progress in solving a problem or overcoming an obstacle, establishing rapport is an essential first step.

Building rapport goes beyond body language; it encompasses style of language and understanding the other party's expectations of a situation.

Being nice and sympathetic is of course important. Most people would agree that it is easier to relate to a person who is polite and courteous. While everyone might prefer to do business with pleasant people, you cannot hope to be that fortunate every time.

Should you have to deal with a person who has an authoritative/ aggressive style, assertive behaviour on your part will be necessary to establish rapport in this situation. The other party may regard you as weak and tractable and do his/her best to override you. To make any progress in an exchange such as this you will find a display of strength more productive.

Developing rapport does not mean agreeing with someone else's point of view. It is about being able to create an atmosphere where discussion can take place openly, so that challenges can be explored without bitterness or rancour. This is one means of positively influencing the way forward to effect a mutually satisfactory outcome.

In NLP mind and body are part of the same system. What occurs in one part will affect all the other parts. In NLP operational principles, you should know what outcome you want to achieve; have sufficient sensory acuity (clear understanding) to deduce whether you are moving away from, or towards your desired goal and have sufficient flexibility of behaviour so that you can vary the way you act until you achieve your objective.

Conversations are often hard to maintain above the level of background noise in many modern venues, so try to be audible rather than loud. Speaking slowly and clearly is better than shouting.

There is no need to feel insignificant when talking to others who are more brilliant or experienced than yourself. Remember emotional intelligence stands you in good stead whether you have first class academic qualifications or not. If you can keep a calm exterior and smooth behaviour you've developed the swan technique. Everyone notices the head and long neck and doesn't see the frantic paddling beneath the water line.

One of the best ways to develop good rapport with someone you've just met is to start by asking a non-threatening question. Open questions are better than something likely to produce a Yes/ No answer. Even an enquiry as simple as 'How far did you have to travel to get here?' is an opening conversational gambit. Be animated – this can be simply a matter of varying your vocal tone. An expressive voice which has warmth and confidence encourages a response from others.

Perhaps you are naturally curious? People who have a genuine interest in others are good at drawing them out. They devise a number of ways of doing this, such as:

- simply offering to do something for them (this need not be anything earth-shattering);
- ask if you can get them a drink if you are at a function;
- help with an introduction to someone you know who they might like to meet;
- give them a piece of helpful information (a good local restaurant, the easiest route to a place).

If your mind goes blank, ask for someone's business card. This will at least give you the opportunity to address them by name and ask them something concerning their work or company location. If you're feeling unsure, watch others in action and emulate those you admire (modelling). You can always learn from any situation, however experienced you are. If someone else's actions make you cringe with embarrassment, at least you've seen how not to do something.

Keeping your eyes and ears open is important. It heightens awareness and you will observe what is going on, and other people will notice you. Try to relax when you are in company with others. Most social events, even if work related, have been well planned and organized by the hosts. They are not intended as an ordeal to be endured by those attending. Enthusiasm is catching and being positive is attractive. It helps shyness evaporate and you may even enjoy yourself. Remember that a positive intention motivates every behaviour.

Not everyone is at ease in unfamiliar company and there are some ways to handle awkward situations:

- Should you make an embarrassing social gaffe in a meeting or business event, have the courage to admit the fault and apologize. Being upfront and honest can turn a mistake to your advantage.

- Should you be put on the spot by being asked a difficult question which you don't know how to answer, you could try turning it around and asking the person for their own view. When you have listened to their reply, it may help you formulate your own reaction.

- Should someone drop a bombshell in your group, they may be testing your (and others') response. Rather than give them the satisfaction of erupting, suspending reaction is the best remedy. A measured acknowledgement and a response along the lines of 'I think I'll need a bit of time to reflect on this' can save faces and reputations.

- Alternatively you may have to make a diplomatic and tactical withdrawal in order to avoid disaster, in which case fall back on a tried and trusted apology: 'I've just seen my boss beckoning to me, please excuse me I must go.'

Although it may seem easy to say, the more you practice talking to people you are not naturally drawn towards, the more your social and rapport-building skills become natural and flexible. Continually practise wherever you are – in the supermarket, at the gym, when travelling or standing in queues. Should you join any new clubs or associations, make time to talk to other members and take advantage of every opportunity to mix with different types of people. It is you who has control of your mind and therefore the results that you achieve.

In essence, rapport building is an indispensable ability for anyone who wishes to develop their confidence, career, business or social life. It is an essential part of the NLP toolkit because you need this ability in the workplace, where good internal and external relationships are an advantage. At best rapport is having the talent to make contact with a diverse range of people. These connections can then be developed into reciprocal relationships to increase your social network, your career or advance your business.

One of the main reasons why rapport building sometimes has a bad reputation is because people who do not understand the process abuse it, by confusing it with selling products or services or trying to get something for themselves at every opportunity. Those who miss the point about good rapport are easy to spot:

- they attempt to dominate groups or conversations;
- they do not engage in dialogue or show interest in offering help to others;
- they are not naturally curious or sensitive to others' needs.

By keeping in mind the positive benefits of creating rapport you should find the process an enjoyable and a productive one.

Rapport means interacting with others, whether it is for fresh ideas, contacts, information or professional development. Having a plan is essential; if you know what you are trying to achieve you are more likely to get it. Analyse the people you meet, how to handle them and make them feel at ease. Don't assume that the most senior people are the only ones of value. Juniors and people who don't hold positions of importance can be just as worthy. Be organized, be personable and be patient. With practice the rewards are high.

> Making good impressions takes time

Different strokes for different folks

NLP believes that the way people think and their reactions to situations depend on a number of factors. When considering the types of people you'll meet, there are a number of categories into which people fall. On first acquaintance it sometimes saves time if you can identify them fairly quickly.

You could come into contact with 'assertive cold' characters. You may find these people do not want any new friends. Nor are they particularly interested in NLP techniques:

- They could be introverted and rarely welcome approaches from other people.
- Preferring to remain aloof, it isn't easy to penetrate their reserve.

- Don't expect a warm welcome when you meet them.
- But their negativity is not personal.
- You will need to keep a professional manner if you are going to keep the encounter going.
- Best advice is keep to business topics, avoid small talk.
- Change the way you behave to maximize the potential of the meeting.
- Make your opening remarks short and to the point.

If you meet an 'accommodating cold' person, these are several degrees warmer than those previously described. The best way to deal with these types is to:

- Let them take the lead.
- Demonstrate that you are in control of the exchange by listening attentively to them.
- Take note of what they say, and if you need to ask questions, make them concise, factual and open.
- Be firm, polite (as always) but not feel subservient. Your best result will be if you can position yourself as confident, professional and calmly determined.

If you meet an 'accommodating warm' person, you will receive a friendly welcome, but so will everyone else. Their warmth doesn't indicate that you are special or are likely to get any closer to them than others:

- Allow them to express their feelings with some small talk initially.
- Stay in command of the conversation yourself.
- If you are talking to this type of person for business reasons keep to the point.
- Should the exchange be allowed to meander off into other directions it will be difficult to steer it back on course because these people are friendly and enjoy talking about almost anything.

- Keep the conversation lively but focused.
- Make sure they register you as a friendly and personable contact.

If you are talking to someone who is an 'assertive warm' character, they will be professional and correct in their exchange and astute:

- If your opening remarks are short, businesslike and clear you will get their attention.
- Indicate why you wanted to meet them.
- Their assertiveness means that they will have a number of ideas that interest them.

> You will get their attention more easily if your opening remarks are short

- Standard responses and approaches may not work here.
- Be prepared to think on your feet during this exchange.
- Keep clearly focused on what you wish to achieve.

Developing rapport with like-minded people is your aim. Similar people to you are going to think and react in a way you'll find easy to deal with. One way is to make a rule to help them as much as they may in time be able to help you. In NLP over and over again you will find that being flexible is paramount. It's not advisable to compartmentalize your colleagues, contacts or acquaintances too firmly. People are spontaneous and liable to change, so if you avoid being judgemental and don't put people in boxes you will be open to opportunities as they occur. People are not always their words and behaviour.

One essential factor in rapport building is motivation. Keep it live, keep it real. If you lose interest in the process, everything can fall apart fairly swiftly. If apathy prevails, nothing will happen. There has to be an incentive to encourage you to continue your rapport building. This comes down to your own personal attitude. You will do best where you feel most comfortable. In an atmosphere where you can relax you will be alert and open to making good contact with other people.

CASE STUDY

Recently a friend invited me to attend a reception. Unfortunately on that particular evening illness prevented her from being there, but she urged me to go along anyway. I did what a lot of people dread, and walked into a room full of strangers. However the venue was luxurious, the drinks and canapés were of the highest quality, the serving staff polite and attentive. I relaxed, thought this isn't all bad, and turned to talk to the man on my right. To break the ice, I asked him what he did. He said he'd retired last year from a career in teaching. I enquired where he'd taught and he named a few schools, one of which I knew. I told him a friend of mine worked there. He was amazed to find that my friend was a man he'd known for over 25 years and he'd even been best man at his wedding. That coincidence was as unexpected as it was extraordinary. People respond according to their internal maps of reality. Luckily I redrew mine on that occasion, otherwise I might have missed the encounter.

If you think it will be difficult to master the art of creating rapport, here are a few tips:

- First, work out the best way to approach people (letter, e-mail, personal meeting).

- What's your purpose? Try to communicate appropriately in any given situation.

- Start by asking them a question; after your enquiry listen carefully to their response.

> Develop an attitude of curiosity towards other people

- Develop an attitude of curiosity towards other people. If you offer assistance to others first, you can then subsequently ask for help or advice.

- When enquiring about something from someone, be attentive and aware. Always keep alert to the opportunities that might present themselves.

- Remember, in business, where friendship isn't always possible, keep an open mind to any possibilities of alliances that might be formed. These can often add value to projects and potential future business.

Nurture new relationships, then watch them prosper

Learn to appreciate other people however different their age and abilities to yours. If you can dispassionately analyse situations this is a huge advantage. Avoid being judgemental and try to be adaptable to other people's needs. Business effectiveness often depends as much on technical skills as human-related activities, relationships, interpersonal skills and communication. This involves the ability to create rapport between parties. You could encounter someone with whom you instantly feel rapport, but unless you follow up on this and spend time talking to them, the relationship will not prosper.

If you want to be an expert in rapport, try to make use of every opportunity to get to know people better.

Make time for face-to-face meetings and encourage chance en-counters. These days it is far too easy to phone, text or e-mail people. These are often the quickest and simplest ways to keep in contact when everyone is so busy and short of time. But where rapport building is concerned, one-to-one encounters are best. They help develop the relationship quickly and easily. But this is also where it is possible to go wrong – the responsibility for building rapport relies on the communicator getting things right.

Clarity and appropriateness are important. Checking your inten-tions is also vital. Ask yourself: 'Why am I doing this?' What is your response? Perhaps you simply don't know. If you are vague about whom you are talking to and what about, have a rethink.

Ask yourself the following questions: What does this person know about me? How much detail should I give them? What sort of reaction do I want to have as a result of this exchange? How is it to be done? How do I want them to feel afterwards: in agreement, pleased, enthusiastic? Be clear. If you can be clear in your own mind as to why something is being done, and you have set yourself defined objectives (you want to know where were they working before they joined the company, or why have they just bought that particular make of car), then plan how you are going to open the exchange.

In each situation a number of different reasons will influence the chosen method of communication: urgency, complexity, formality, involvement of a number of other parties, etc. Every possible method of approach needs to be considered.

Remember, a face-to-face meeting may not be everyone's favourite activity, even if you think they are great. For some people, who would much rather send an e-mail, they may be an ordeal. No doubt many of you will have spent hours of your precious time in pointless conversations where little useful information is exchanged or discussed. You may have a healthy dislike of meetings because a number you have had to attend were badly run or ill-prepared.

Person to person exchanges are like any other meeting, they can be used to:

- inform, analyse and solve problems;
- discuss and exchange views;
- inspire and motivate;
- counsel and reconcile conflict;
- obtain opinion and feedback;
- persuade;
- reinforce the status quo;
- instigate change in knowledge, skills or attitudes.

These exchanges are potentially useful because it is only by continued contact with someone can you reach close rapport. When you meet someone face to face, remember to use the time wisely (because they may be very busy and you won't have very long). Do you want to inform or update them on something? Are you anxious to canvass their opinion? Do you wish to involve them in a project or event?

Are you hoping to invite them to a social gathering? Do you want them to be made aware of your presence for some reason?

Whatever the reason for seeking a face-to-face encounter with someone, it is important to get off to a good start. Be positive, ensure that your purpose is clear, and establish your authority by engaging the other person's interest. Make sure the atmosphere is right – friendly and flexible, but keep a professional yet informal manner. Always keep a limit on the time, respecting other people's schedules.

To create rapport with another person successfully, two-way communication is essential. You will need to encourage your contact to communicate with you, whether you want to:

- build a relationship;
- exchange ideas and suggestions;
- invite comments or feedback.

You should also:

- keep in touch by a variety of means; eg provide regular pieces of relevant information or feedback for them;
- react positively and acknowledge and thank them at each and every exchange;
- where possible give credit, as this will ensure a flow of ideas and further exchanges;
- try to be available for a short time, even if you are busy, when someone approaches you.

Being in rapport with someone and having a relationship with someone are not the same thing. To help you distinguish between them, consider the following. Someone wanting to establish rapport with another person may not wish, or need, to develop a relationship with them.

Say you are having to cope with some challenging building contractors who are working at your house; it's sensible to develop rapport with them. Why? At the very least so that you can be fairly certain that they will turn up for work each day until they've finished the job that they're contracted for.

You may have already mentally resolved never to use that company again, yet establishing harmonious dealings with them while they carry out the repairs to your home is prudent. Dealing with them politely may mean their behaviour is more measured (less noise and mess perhaps). You will be less stressed if you treat them more reasonably than they're treating you; they could (possibly) begin to match and mirror your behaviour.

However, once they've finished the work on your house, you may wish never to set eyes on them again, in which case the need to develop rapport with them is a means to an end. It is for a sole purpose, not to try to build a relationship. By using NLP-related techniques (matching, mirroring – as mentioned earlier) it is possible to establish rapport with someone within a very short space of time. This rapport, in turn, may also exist for a very short space of time. This does not make it any less valid.

Rapport building, as explained, is not a continuous process. Relationship building, on the other hand, is. Developing a relationship with someone is different – it implies an ongoing process. Indeed it is possible to have a relationship with someone with whom you may no rapport whatsoever. There are many people who have difficult relatives whom they encounter on a regular basis at family gatherings. If we're honest most of us have one or two people in our lives (an irritating neighbour, a high-maintenance acquaintance, a needy colleague) who crop up on a fairly regular basis. The issue here is not to try to develop rapport with them because there's possibly no requirement, but to accept the relationship exists and minimize the aggravation each encounter causes. Those to whom it comes naturally often have the following attributes:

- they treat everyone as being interesting, special and likeable;
- they use good eye contact and positive body language;
- they make other people, particularly new acquaintances, feel safe and relaxed whatever the occasion;
- they are at ease when introducing people to each other;
- they make an effort to remember names and something relevant about everyone they meet.

Have you met anyone recently whom you found easy to get on with? Chances are they had charisma. When you were introduced, did they smile, enter into conversation easily and draw you out? They probably asked you questions about yourself, and listened to what you said. In essence, they made you feel important. When you parted, you probably thought what a great person they were. Not only were they at ease with themselves, they made you feel relaxed in their company.

People who become skilled at relationship building or who have natural rapport integrate this into their lives. They maintain contact with lots of people on a regular basis, they exchange ideas, information and offer help. You may know people who do this, or maybe you are one of them. Their outstanding characteristics include sincerity, curiosity, consideration, sharing, understanding and appreciation. They tend to be 'givers' rather than 'takers'. They keep in touch with their contacts even though there is seemingly 'nothing in it for them'. They are always open to opportunities to assist people and to broaden their range of contacts by sharing and exchanging information. In other words they don't think time spent building relationships is wasted, rather it gives them endless opportunities to learn new things.

Chapter 08
Influencing skills are better than status

How to get exactly what you want

For those who want to get the most out of situations and are keen to employ NLP skills, there is nothing more important than becoming an expert influencer. People who are persuasive are able to negotiate and exert influence on others. One thing they all know how to do is continually to adapt their behaviour to obtain the most desirable outcome in a situation or exchange. This doesn't mean that they will automatically achieve their objective, but they will be in control of the process. They should be able, by flexible behaviour, to lead the other party towards a satisfactory conclusion.

In NLP the influences that affect people's thinking and reactions to situations depend on various things. Some of these factors are external and some are internal. As mentioned earlier, external factors could be your environment (where you work, live or socialize), other people's behaviour (or emotions), what other people say, how they look and what their intentions are. The internal factors could be all or any of the following: your role, identity and capability in a particular context, your beliefs and values, the purpose you have in mind, and your perceptions and preconceptions, your emotions.

Any encounter is a two-way process. When using influencing skills, the person with whom you are interacting will want to feel important and to be respected. They will want their needs to be considered, and they will need to feel able to trust you. They will require

> Any encounter is
> a two-way process

input or ideas from you and to be made aware of any difficult issues or problems as they arise. This may seem a bit of a tall order, but unless you are professional, reliable, discreet and honest, you will not be able to influence or persuade others.

It may be impossible to know yourself completely, but when trying to be an influencer, being aware of your personal strengths, weaknesses, hang-ups and prejudices is a great help. What are your attitudes and values? If you know what they are, you will be able to adapt your own traits so that you can influence others without your own behaviour hindering the process.

Why become an influencer?

Some of the benefits of becoming an effective influencer are: it proves you are flexible enough to cope with change; you are able to motivate others and improve morale amongst staff; you can develop and build strong work teams; you can involve others and get their commitment; you can obtain greater levels of respect from others; increased self-confidence.

Interaction between parties requires perception and sensitivity. Influencing others is something best achieved by being alert in mind, emotion and body. The ability to concentrate well is also an advantage. You want to start a process where you can achieve a desirable outcome (for both parties). This requires a competent performance and for this you will need confidence.

People show confidence in different ways. Some are robust and self-assured; others may be risk-takers and seek out challenging situations. Every person will react differently and each encounter will be unique and present different opportunities for your influencing skills. If you are resourceful and adaptable, you won't need a script to work from. The ability to influence others is a bit like dancing. Each step needs to be taken willingly, in tandem with another party, before moving on to the next one. If you are trying to lead your prospective partner on to the floor to do the tango, make sure they're not expecting to dance a waltz. Confusion with the footwork leads to a tangled heap on the floor, which will be embarrassing for everyone.

In practical terms: what does influencing mean? In order to answer that you need to know what you want to achieve. You also need to know whether, realistically, you can achieve it. Successful influencing is about what you can achieve. But most importantly, influencing is about creating movement. When trying to influence a situation one way or another, you do not have to have continuous movement. A pause often comes in useful. In NLP it is impossible not to communicate – even if you are doing nothing. It is a powerful tactic as it allows time to assess progress and regroup.

However, the influencing process needs to be balanced; each party should be open in negotiation, able to weigh up the pros and cons of information exchanged before making a decision to take a further step forward. No exchange is ever perfect, neither is it possible to assess how quickly or easily your objective will be achieved. It's true, the old saying: 'More haste, less speed'. As long as a positive balance is maintained, progress will be made.

There are various ways to influence people and a number of different styles can be used, to greater or lesser effect. Remember in NLP success depends on varying what you do until you get the result that you want. You could use charm to influence people. Or you could use compelling information. You could use the art of compromise or negotiation. You could use an emotional appeal. You could use coercion tactics.

Say the plan (on your part) is to influence someone to award a major contract to a particular organization. Then the success or failure of it could have dramatic consequences for a large number of people. It could include other parties involved in the decision-making process, or competitors (of yours) also putting on a charm offensive for similar reasons. As long as you remember that this process is inherently two-way, and that satisfaction is needed on both sides for it to continue, then you will be able to make progress towards a winning outcome.

It always helps to have a plan, a structured approach. Sometimes it can resemble a map. Even if you have to deviate from the arranged route, the chart should help you keep as close to your chosen path as possible. The overall process of influencing other people and situations is multifaceted. It needs to be controlled and it needs to be managed.

There is a five-step strategy that can be used in some situations to influence people or outcomes. It is structured and forceful. Step 1 – Set the scene; Step 2 – Invite reactions; Step 3 – Summarize; Step 4 – Deal with objections; Step 5 – Agree outcomes.

Sometimes the above steps just don't work because they are too rigid, in which case a change of tactic might help. There is a more liberal version. Step 1 – State your view of the problem; Step 2 – Clarify others' views; Step 3 – Work towards agreement; Step 4 – Look for a win–win situation; Step 5 – Achieve joint agreement. The key factors in achieving a successful outcome are the quality of the questions used (to test understanding and elicit information) and the ability to build upon ideas and proposals.

In any complex process where there is a need to relate closely to someone (or more than one), this can best be done if it is thought through carefully and approached in a planned and structured way. Effectively you are trying to play an influential part in the other people's decision-making processes. Your objective is to assist them to make the decision – the right one – that will have the result of giving you your desired outcome. The more you are prepared to 'give', the more likely you are to achieve your goal. This is why the second approach often succeeds.

Critical success factors

If you play to your own unique strengths to help nurture the process, this will get you off to a good start. Try to keep in mind the importance of seeing things from 'the other side's point of view'. Fine-tuning is paramount; being able to deploy appropriate approaches from all your available interpersonal skills (discussed in the chapter on 'Rapport') is advantageous. You will learn something from every encounter, even if it's how not to do it in future. In NLP don't think 'failure', think 'opportunity to learn'.

To put this in perspective, reflect for a moment on the last four influential exchanges you had. Why were they important? Was it for professional or personal reasons? What do you remember about the encounters? What did the other person say? How did they say it? Did you understand what they meant? Did they understand you? Did you agree or disagree on something? If it was the latter, what could have been changed (during the meeting) so that your viewpoints did not differ? What was the outcome? Was it successful from each angle? Did you achieve your objective?

Try to get into the habit of reviewing each meeting in your mind after you've finished. Only through feedback and situation analysis will you learn from the experience. You will need to think about your style of approach: Were you correct in your assessment of the current situation? Did your way of influencing others seem appropriate? Were you able to watch others' influencing behaviour? Were you influenced by their methods?

Being open and flexible in the way you communicate with other people will avoid you repeating any mistakes. Your approaches will appear fresh and well directed in future. In the context of business dealings, always prepare. Good planning is one way to give yourself an advantage over any other parties. Success depends on varying what you do until you get the result you want.

This does not have to be a huge exercise: just taking a few minutes to think matters through before you begin to speak to someone will help. If it is an important meeting which could have significant results for your company, canvassing the opinion of a couple of colleagues about how you should display your hand might be worthwhile. They may have knowledge of the other party that you do not and which could give you an edge.

For example, you may be meeting someone who is very busy. The less of his or her time you take up will earn you valuable points. Don't spend ten minutes describing the awful traffic conditions you encountered on your journey to the meeting. Likewise, if a 'warm-up' session is necessary to put the other party at their ease, spend a few minutes in small talk. You could enquire about their favourite hobby, or if they enjoyed the latest sporting event (football match, cricket test match). Be sensitive to their reactions.

If you can set your objectives before you plunge into an exchange you will feel more confident. You should be able to relax and enjoy the process. If you go unprepared and you don't know where you are heading, how will you know when you get there? One way of looking at the art of influencing others is to regard it as a journey. Make sure you start from the best place. Two people will see things in entirely different ways.

Each interface will need clear objectives: do you want to do some new business? Do you want the person to be an 'influencer' on your own personal behalf? Perhaps you are trying to obtain a certain piece of information, or hoping to work for their organization at some point in the future. Would you like them to introduce you to an influential person they know? If you don't have a clear idea of what you are trying to do, it is difficult to know what behaviour is best to employ in order to achieve it.

There is a well-known mnemonic that is attributable in many situations. When you are trying to influence someone, it is better if your objectives are SMART:

- Specific: be clear about what you want to achieve.

- Measurable: identify the stages so you can track progress.

- Achievable: can you really do it? Be honest, not overambitious.

- Realistic: should you actually be starting this process. Is it the right time for you (and your company)? Have you identified the right party?

- Time-based: work out in advance when you expect to achieve your desired outcome – days/weeks/months/years?

Do it first, do it right, do it continuously

If you are naturally observant, you may be able to create opportunities to influence other parties that could otherwise easily be missed. When scanning your local paper or professional journals, always keep an eye on pieces of news about people you know. Someone may have won an award for a new project, or raised money for a local charity. Use the opportunity to get in touch with them and say how pleased you were to see them mentioned in the news. They will be flattered and remember that you took the time to contact them. By being observant and courteous, they will remember you. This will be to your advantage should you need to seek their help or advice in future.

There is no 'best time' to be an influencer, or to put your skills to the test. Some people prefer to be contacted during working hours, but with flexible work patterns on the increase it is often easier to make contact with people at other times. Should someone you have been trying to reach say they can only speak to you at the weekend, try to be available and flexible. By fitting in with their timetable it shows you are sympathetic and able to accommodate others' needs. This gives you an advantage over people who are more rigid in their dealings.

The ability to influence other people isn't something you can do in a hurry. It takes time, patience and perseverance. All good relationships are built over time and once in place are difficult to dislodge. If a relationship has secure foundations, it will endure the hiccups and glitches that are part of everyday life. You might think that the person you have just met is an ideal party who will be easy to influence to your way of thinking. But decisions made on the instant don't always turn out to be best.

Do you remember the story of the three little pigs? They built their houses out of straw, wood and bricks. The houses built of straw and wood were quick to construct, but they blew away equally fast when the wolf arrived and they offered little or no protection to their occupants. Should you be able to persuade someone to do something easily and quickly, be aware that they may change their mind. This would make your effort worthless, so taking things slowly does pay dividends in many cases.

It's often the thought that counts where influencing skills are concerned. It's not a bad idea to get personal, in appropriate circumstances. If, for example, you have got to know someone over a period of time, remembering their birthday, or asking after their family (including mentioning their child's name) will register with them. They will feel that you are interested in them as a person, not just because of the job they do or position they hold.

To harness the skills required to become an expert influencer, keep the following tips in mind: persistence pays, there is no doubt about that. Consider that the ability to influence others is like planting a seed, it takes time to germinate. One of the most important factors in the process is preparation. The more you know about the person (or situation) you are trying to influence, the more likely you are to succeed. You may need to exercise patience, but always be polite. A positive mental attitude and outlook is infectious and persuasive. All the above tactics get easier with practice. Don't underestimate the value of praise when communicating with other people. Most people respond positively to flattery.

If you want to acquire the art of persuasion, often using words is not enough. You have to be able to hook the other party into the idea that there is something in it for them. Once they accept this, you are more likely to be able to influence them in the way you seek. To be persuasive you should offer people reasons that reflect their point of view. You won't be influential at all if you just tell them why they should do something.

Benefits are things that do something for people. The benefits of reading this book include the fact that at the end of this chapter you will have the power to influence people and situations in a way that you want. Making your view understandable, by explaining issues in a simple way, would be a benefit. If you are dealing on a professional level, make sure your communication is factual and efficient. If you want to sound friendly, more informal and approachable, make your approach match the message you wish to convey.

It is said that people act on emotion and justify with logic. To be an effective persuader you should not only offer good reasons for something but also create emotional goodwill at the same time. If you need to influence powerfully, bring in stories to connect with people's hearts as well as minds. If your objective was to influence someone to donate organs or blood, you could tell them a story about a friend who nearly died but was saved by a generous donor. Perhaps you have noticed that successful fundraisers tend to use emotive illustrations to persuade people to give huge sums of money to charities. Their ability to influence people via their appeals can bring in thousands of pounds in revenue.

If at first you don't succeed, call in reinforcements. A friendly helper may be all that is needed. Recommendations work wonders when you are trying to persuade someone to take a particular course of action. Try this: if you and the other party have a mutual friend or colleague, ask them to act as an independent influencer. Someone who confirms that you have already helped them in some way or other will give the other party proof of your sound judgement and reasoning. You will find it much easier to influence them as a result.

If it's really important, don't rely on just one source for recommendations. Using several different parties gives even further weight to your case. You increase your chances of success in that one or other of your sources may be a powerful influence over the person with whom you are interacting.

Chapter 09
Learning:
the most effective
ways to do it

Learning is behind everything NLP teaches, as it is essentially about gaining insights and knowledge that enable us to understand and use our words and behaviour to convert information into meaning.

There are numerous, often contradictory, theories about learning. It remains a highly active and continuously developing area for debate. NLP is not so much concerned about theories of learning as about how learning is applied. A central tenet, as mentioned previously, is the acquisition of knowledge and skill by reference to those who may be experts or notable examples in a particular field. But that is just one technique.

In simple terms, there are three ways to learn. These are through behaviour, where you learn by doing things; awareness, where you learn from what you observe, hear and feel (including how other people do things); and process, where you work things out as, for example, in solving problems.

The principal catalysts for learning are fear, fun, conformity, competition, conflict, hunger, curiosity and ambition. There is also ambient learning, where information is automatically filtered and absorbed because it is impossible to ignore its existence. So, for example, if you are driving through the countryside and there are green hills in front of you, even though you are concentrating on something else, you will be aware of the presence of 'green' and the presence of hills.

The starting point for learning is the conscious or unconscious knowledge you already have. The learning process takes place through applying new knowledge to an existing framework. You cannot learn in a vacuum.

Depending on their personalities and experience, people have different learning styles that suit them best, but there are general observations that hold good for most people. The sections below illustrate different ways of learning and how they relate to NLP.

If you ever had to learn theorems at school (a theorem is a chain of algebraic arguments to support a geometric proposition) you will probably know, and may have experienced, that there is a hard way and an easy way. If your teacher told you just to learn them, as many did, then chances are that you would have done so laboriously by rote. If, rather than being told to 'learn' them you were told to 'work them out' based on a set of geometric truths of which you were already aware, it would have been a much simpler and quicker task and previous learning would have been reinforced. It would have been the efficient application of existing knowledge to new learning compared to memorizing a long sequence of codes.

Anecdote and analogy provide great learning 'hooks'

Anecdote and analogy are powerful tools to convey meaning. For example, military strategy can be used to inform business strategy as similar principles apply. Military strategy is the analogy. A useful anecdote to help an early-stage business might be the beachhead strategy employed by British forces to recapture the Falkland Islands in 1982. The challenge was for around 5,000 British personnel, mostly seasick on ships, to displace 10,000 Argentinian personnel dug into trenches at strategic points on the island. Rather than try to land front on, the strategy was to land a small force at an entirely unexpected location, to land a second and then others close by, consolidate forces and 'yomp' over to Argentinian positions from the rear. An early-stage business with limited resources, rather than confront powerful competitors full on would be advised to adopt a beachhead, or niche strategy to gain a foothold in the market and progress from the position of relative strength established but in a small area – the big fish, small pond syndrome.

A further example of useful analogy is the use of Shakespeare in relating to business principles. One particular publication is *The Bard & Co: Shakespeare's Role in Modern Business* (edited by Jim Davies, John Simmons and Rob Williams), which has lots of stories that can instantly be converted into a business context.

The NLP principle in each case is the communication of the known to make the unknown more easily accessible.

Collaborative working boosts everyone's performance

Collaboration creates a mutually supportive learning environment and accelerates the process of learning compared to doing it on your own. Although the reason for learning in classes is mostly about economies of scale, if used properly and not solely the 'chalk and talk' method is applied, there will be a multiplier effect on the learning process. In teaching English to overseas students, a principle often applied to create a learning pattern involves: 'teacher to student, student to student, student to teacher', where the teacher utters a phrase in English, one student utters the same phrase to another and the other repeats that phrase back to the teacher, thus creating a loop of communication that can be repeated until any issues have been ironed out. Although that is somewhat of an over-simplification, a real-life example of a similar principle at work achieved exceptional results and is described below.

CASE STUDY

A six-stream comprehensive school in Southampton asked an English teaching specialist if he would teach a mathematics class during the following year. The teacher concerned did not want to do it and explained that he had badly failed his own mathematics exams at school, having gained a poor grade 8 (out of 9) in his General Certificate of Education. Because there were no other staff who could be allocated this responsibility it had to be accepted, however. The class in question was a mixed sex fourth stream of 13–14-year-olds – not the easiest of groups to teach under the best of circumstances.

On the first day of term, the teacher introduced himself to the class and commiserated with them that they had him to contend with for a year. He was lousy at maths and would need their help if they were to learn very much. Unaccustomed to this frank approach, the pupils agreed that they would help if it was necessary but were not sure what to expect. In the event, when the teacher was having difficulty explaining how to multiply fractions, one of the pupils said: 'That's not the best way to do it sir; would you like me to explain it my way?' He went up to the front and duly explained it to the class who, to the teacher's surprise, grasped it immediately.

Following this welcome intervention, the class was asked if it thought it could do as well as the stream above it (with a proper maths teacher) going through the identical syllabus 'if we all cooperated'. Members of the class were not sure but said that it would be worth trying.

In the event, those better at the subject worked with the groups of the less able, speaking their language, exercising surprising patience and helping them to learn.

Not only did this class equal the performance of the higher stream, average marks came out appreciably higher. Working collaboratively, the pupils performed considerably better than if 'taught' by a less than fully competent teacher.

NLP principles at work in the above example show pupils with similar knowledge and experiences being able to communicate effectively on their terms and not those of the teacher. The rapport established between the pupils might not otherwise have been so strong. The whole group's orientation towards a specific outcome and a preparedness to behave in a different way, in order to achieve it, added momentum to the process. Pupils regarded their ill-qualified teacher, not as a problem but as a positive challenge that they could overcome.

Trial and error learning: sounds risky but works well

When you move to a new town or even country location, it can be initially confusing trying to find your way around. Progressively you become familiar with some routes and then others until eventually you have sufficient knowledge not to get lost. Learning is supported by the sight of physical landmarks that reconfirm to you that you are in one specific place compared to another. In all likelihood, that is how you would give directions to visitors. Eventually you will have a 'map' in your head in order to navigate any journey you choose. Although the process ends up with an internal map, starting with that map would not have been so easy. You have to go through a process of trial and error before appreciating your 'field of operation'.

As mentioned previously, in experiments with rats that have to negotiate a maze before they can reach the food that they know is at the end of it, there is a 'field cognition' learning process. Learning by this method leads instinctively to knowing where you are going and imprints this knowledge for the long term.

Learning by association means that one thing leads to another

As with the earlier example of Pavlov's dogs, certain things, activities and events become associated with particular stimuli. Those stimuli may be sounds, smells, sights, tastes or tactile experiences. The dogs associated the ringing of a bell with food. You might associate a particular scent with your grandmother's sitting room, which in turn leads you to recall other memories. The taste of a particular kind of coffee might bring back memories of an overseas holiday. The sight of the dentist's chair may bring back fearful childhood memories. Learning by association is about triggers – just think of the lines your children might shout back to a clown at a pantomime or other stage performance. Learning by association is particularly good for routines and processes. It fits with the NLP model in that it uses one idea to evoke another and leads to a predetermined action.

Other ways to remember things: the value of aide-memoires or mnemonics

In the modern world of business and public service, we are beset by TLAs. That's 'three-letter acronyms' to you and me. They are supposed to streamline communication and make things easier to recall. At a computer trade show in the late 1970s, 62 out of fewer than 120 exhibitors were companies branded with three-letter acronyms. Apart from IBM, none of them has remained memorable and most are no longer in business. It is very few brands that make their mark on the basis of a set of initials; 3M, GE, BP, BT are exceptions whose recall is made easier as they are so frequently encountered.

Acronyms can however be a very powerful aid to learning. AIDA is an acronym that helps marketers devise persuasive texts to support their products and services. It is also very helpful in following a process for giving sales presentations. It is based on the premise that if you want people to buy from you, you must first say something that commands their 'Attention'. Having engaged their attention, the next step is to arouse their 'Interest'. From being just interested you then want to encourage their 'Desire'. Finally, you want them to take some 'Action'. It is a very simple model but gives a structure that is logical and, above all, works.

Other mnemonics use representational sentences with which another set of meanings is associated. To remember the colours of the rainbow in the right order is made far easier by first remembering and then applying the sentence 'Richard Of York Gave Battle In Vain' to denote red, orange, yellow, green, blue, indigo and violet.

These days we all have to remember PIN numbers, security codes, passwords and maybe even favourite lottery numbers. The postcode suffix 4UE was remembered as 'For Hughў' which it sounds like if you drop the 'H'. This in turn was code for the sound of being sick after too much drink! Security codes on a keypad could be remembered by the physical pattern of the digits or through birth dates. Similarly, passwords usually attach themselves to something familiar that you can more easily recall. We all make a lot of use of mnemonics and when communicating it makes a lot of sense to create memory hooks to maximize what others will respond to and retain in their minds.

In a business context, there are various aide-memoires that can be used in order to apply management and operational principles without having to rely on memorizing detail. Some of these, including AIDA, are listed below:

Sample aide-memoires

A manager's role can be summarized as being responsible for four areas:

> ACTIVITIES
> PEOPLE
> RESOURCES
> INFORMATION

An interviewer will need to test five attributes to recruit successfully:

> KNOWLEDGE
> SKILLS
> QUALIFICATIONS
> EXPERIENCE
> ATTITUDE – THIS IS THE MOST
> IMPORTANT

In setting objectives, they should be SMART:

> **SPECIFIC**
> **MEASURABLE**
> **ACHIEVABLE**
> **RELEVANT**
> **TIME-BASED**

In order to prioritize your use of time you should consider whether what you have to do is:

> **IMPORTANT AND URGENT**
> **IMPORTANT, BUT NON-URGENT**
> **NOT IMPORTANT, BUT URGENT**
> **NOT IMPORTANT, NOR URGENT**

In order to persuade someone, your communication should use the AIDA sequence in seeking the better likelihood of a result:

> **ATTENTION**
> **INTEREST**
> **DESIRE**
> **ACTION**

Conflicting ideas: how tensions in the mind create a strong learning incentive

A powerful aid to learning is to create conflicting thoughts in someone's mind that cause them to concentrate on what is really meant and to resolve the dilemma. In other words, if we communicate the unexpected, there is a tension between that and what was expected. People use such 'dissonance' in advertising so that the images created will stick in the mind. Many years ago, *The Times* published an advertisement featuring a pregnant man. At the time, this was very controversial and widely debated. It significantly multiplied the impact of an otherwise ordinary advertising proposition.

When a branch of the UK Womens Institute (WI) published a calendar featuring members in the nude it was entirely contrary to the perceived ethos of that organization and the expected attitudes of the women in such an august body. People have learned much more about the WI as a result.

Learning is about the retention of knowledge, and something dissonant or conflicting heightens the likelihood of that retention. Being introduced to Rousseau's views on education was given greater focus and therefore a hook to further learning by the pronouncement that 'Rousseau invented the child'.

In its simplest terms, a child learns through touching something hot that it should not be touched again. Our mistakes cause us internal conflict that acts as an incentive to getting it right next time. In NLP terms, dissonance heightens interest and the likelihood of a communication being retained in the memory as it forces people to consider and extract real meaning.

In a sales environment it is a frequently observed phenomenon that someone who wins a big, hard fought-for sale, after an initial feeling of elation, feels rather depressed. This has been described as 'cognitive dissonance' as it is the opposite to what one would usually expect in these circumstances until you realize that the sales person has to find a new focus now that the challenge has been removed. So it means starting all over again.

Choice of words, together with scope and sequence profoundly affect meaning

Words can never be perfect in representing meaning as they are just the code to describe an idea or experience and not the experience itself. The choice of words used needs to be sufficiently close to the vocabulary and experience of the recipient if he or she is to receive the information in the way it was intended. This book, for example, has been written to be mostly free of the vocabulary that NLP specialists use amongst themselves. This is so that it will be more accessible to readers who do not possess that vocabulary. It is intended to convey NLP principles, beliefs and techniques in a language that most of us already understand. This is to make the learning process a single as compared to double step and is therefore expected to be easier to digest.

In learning English, if you are first required to differentiate between verbs, adverbs, nouns, adjectives, prepositions, clauses, phrases, synonyms and antonyms as well as different tenses, you will be slower to pick up the vocabulary of the language itself. This has been well proven by the direct method, used in foreign language teaching, that rapidly gives people a good working vocabulary against which they can subsequently build the right technical language structure.

Understanding people's capacity and the scope of the information that they can absorb in particular circumstances is also critical to the success of any piece of communication.

The surprising importance of guesswork

Using guesswork seems to be at odds with the notion of arriving at a clear outcome yet is an important tool in the process. George Pólya, the famous Hungarian mathematician and author of the best-selling book *How to Solve It* said: 'To be a good mathematician, or a good gambler, or good at anything, you must be a good gambler.'

It is often difficult for companies to develop strategies for the future because they have no real idea what the future will hold and cannot therefore calculate how to get there. When this is the case, rather than abandoning the attempt, it is more productive to come up with what you could regard as a 'synthetic' idea. That is to say 'have a stab' at something that you might feel comfortable with if it were real.

You may have no idea whether or not you could double in size, dominate the market or a market niche, expand into three continents and retire a millionaire. However, if you do set those as synthetic goals, you have a good chance of working out what would need to happen in order that, however improbably, they could be achieved. If you work out what would need to happen, you are then in a position where you would know what the first step would be. If you know the first one, it is then easier to calculate the second, and so on. If you take the steps one at a time and do not try to jump ahead of the process, you will progressively succeed.

This is entirely consistent with NLP operating principles that first ask you to envisage an outcome, develop a route to achieving that outcome and adapt to circumstances as they occur until you find the best of the options. You then drive through until the outcome is achieved.

NLP says that people have all the resources they need to achieve what they want and that the real barrier is a lack of belief rather than a lack of personal resources. The same applies to organizations. History has countless examples of how people and businesses have been successful, apparently against all the odds.

In a learning context, going through the process as described above leads progressively to better knowledge and understanding, new skills borne out of necessity and the wisdom that comes from experience. This far exceeds any expectations than if there had not been a guess in the first place.

Learning through NLP

If through careful analysis of people's words, physical state and behaviour you can work out what they mean, you will have learned a powerful means by which you can improve your own success in interacting with others. If by using NLP you can influence beneficial change in others, they will also benefit from learning new ways to achieve success in their own and others' lives.

Part Two
NLP and 26 situations or challenges you may face

Chapter 10
Facing management challenges

Recognizing and dealing with bullying

Situation

Bullying is not just about being shouted at, humiliated and threatened. It takes many subtle and complex forms. It is extremely common in the workplace and is as much practised by women as men.

People who are subjected to bullying may be fooled into believing that the reasons they are picked on or criticized are partially due to themselves in some way not being adequate in the role they occupy or the tasks they undertake.

Constant fault-finding, nit-picking, being put down, undermined or simply being ignored are the hallmark of the bully whose purpose, intentional or otherwise, is to increase or reinforce their own self-worth at the expense of yours. They can sometimes isolate you from others and will frequently distort what you do and say.

Bullies will overload you with work, claim credit for your work, set unrealistic goals and block your progress, your time off and your rewards, unless it suits them otherwise. The likelihood of you being given personal development training is remote.

Managers and supervisors who have not been trained for the man-management responsibilities they have been given often assume a stereotype of how they think a manager should behave. Being 'in charge' is more important to them than the development and motivation of others.

Behaviour

> Bullies are selective listeners

Bullies are selective listeners, always superimposing their own interpretation of words and behaviour to suit the way they want to respond. They are more likely to ask you 'What went wrong?' than 'Can you tell me what happened?'

If you request time off for a couple of days they will ask you 'Why do you need that then?', thus giving themselves the opportunity to criticize the reason and therefore the validity of the request and making it easier for them to refuse.

Bullies often speak in generalizations such as 'I'm not happy with that', without giving a specific cause and effect reason for what they are reacting to. They will say 'I haven't got time to waste' midway through an interchange, thus implying, without precisely saying, that their time is more important than yours.

Typically, bullies are also cowards. They fear the opprobrium of their superiors and do everything to impress them. Being 'shown up'

> Typically, bullies are also cowards

is a frequent cause of their anger as they have no concept of the learning potential for them and the individual involved in making the occasional mistake.

Mocking and derision are very powerful means for the bully to make you feel awful and them feel good. This is more often than not done in front of others than to you alone, as it makes the impact more powerful and long lasting.

Body language that displays intolerance, boredom, indifference or scorn can often make otherwise articulate people completely tongue-tied when trying to communicate with someone whose principal purpose is to make you seem irrelevant.

Bullies can sometimes invoke disciplinary procedures in order to force constructive dismissal, early retirement or other form of coercion. They do this believing that they will no doubt be supported by their superiors, who cannot see through their sycophantic ways.

NLP observation

Bullies, because their behaviour undermines rather than supports others, can be seen to be ignoring the positive and harmonizing effect of a number of NLP beliefs and assumptions. They do not observe that a positive intention motivates every behaviour (in the person who is subject to their bullying), they do not modify their maps of the world and they certainly do not replace the word 'failure' with 'opportunity to learn'. They also distort context to suit themselves, but use different contexts with their superiors, so their perceptions will be different.

In dealing with bullies it is important to force them to be specific and detailed so as to remove the emotional element of their position and get their focus on facts and choice of remedies rather than their feelings or their posturing. A supervisor in a clothing factory called up one of the workers to explain why one garment had been incorrectly stitched. She could have waited to be told off, but before he could say anything said 'Shall I go and put it right?' to which he had no alternative than to answer 'Yes'. This removed the opportunity for him to lecture her on not letting the factory down, the importance of standards and so on, and effectively took the wind out of his sails by changing the context.

As NLP envisages changing your behaviour until you find one that enables you to achieve your goal, dealing with bullying may concern more than your stance towards the bully and involve other strategies such as invoking a complaints procedure, changing jobs, taking advice on how to cope or simply eliciting colleagues' support. As long as you imagine yourself to be the victim with the problem, you will remain so. Once you take charge of the situation you can give the bully the problem because you have the inner resourcefulness to do so. Doing nothing solves nothing, so if you want to make change, then you have to take the first step now.

Managing by objectives

Situation

Many organizations are good at managing the tasks of their employees and the operational aspects of the business, but do not necessarily equip staff to make the emotional as well as physical commitment necessary to make the enterprise as successful as it could be. A simple way to test the effectiveness of a good management system is to ask an employee the following ten 'Yes/No' questions:

1 Do you know what the business intends to become?

2 Do you know this year's measures of success?

3 Do you know who contributes what to that success?

4 Do you know clearly what your function contributes?

5 Do you know what you must achieve personally?

6 Do you have access to help and guidance from colleagues?

7 Do you know how you can develop your own role?

8 Do you know the knowledge/skills gaps you can address?

9 Do you have the resources to do the job competently?

10 Are you confident you will be able to make progress?

If the employee is not able to answer 'Yes' to most of the above questions then it is unlikely that he or she can be expected to contribute as fully as possible to the forward momentum of the organization.

When, shortly after taking office, US President Lyndon Johnson was visiting the Cape Kennedy launching site for the US space programme he stopped his motorcade to speak with a man who was in the process of sweeping the approach road to the site. When he asked the man what he was doing, the response came back: 'I'm helping to put a man on the moon, sir.' Although that may to some be a 'cheesy' story, it illustrates the necessary contribution of even the most menial tasks to the main endeavour. If the man had not known why he was sweeping the road and that it was just a task he had been given, there would be no sense of pride and worth to spur him

TABLE 10.1

Name
achievement matrix FOR PERIOD No. Date

Achievements during last period (not a list of activities and actions but just those things that have made a material difference)	**Objectives for next period** (the major things I will do to move the business forward)
1 ▼	4 ◄
Obstacles to achievement (things that have impeded what I have wanted to do)	**Action taken to remove those obstacles**
2 ►	3 ▲

on to do it to the best of his ability. That is why providing a vision and objectives are so important as a management responsibility.

Behaviour

'Mushroom management' is a pejorative expression given to the behaviour of keeping employees in the dark, and showering them with 'manure' in a vain attempt to stimulate their growth and development. Withholding information, although some managers will think it keeps them in control, negates the imagination and initiative that otherwise could be shown by the employee.

Some managers, because they are 'in charge', believe that they are most effective when handing out a series of tasks, and resent employees questioning why. In both cases, what is perceived as strength is really a weakness. The phenomenon is surprisingly common on the factory floor and in traditional businesses such as retail, service and administration where bad habits, through lack of training, have never been properly addressed.

Enlightened managers set, monitor and adjust objectives in order to equip others and manage their performance. Managing by objectives is the opposite to the old-style military management style of command and control.

NLP observation

People are much better than poor managers think they are. Because their own perception is that their superior position confers more skill, know-how and knowledge than those that work for them, they can never fully trust others to use their own initiative and act effectively.

The open-minded, perceptive manager knows that an employee has the ability to attain the necessary skills and knowledge, given opportunity and incentive, and that with experience comes the ability to help the development of others.

> Dictatorial managers lack the ability to establish rapport

Dictatorial managers lack the ability to establish rapport and can therefore never communicate with staff in a way that satisfies either themselves or their reportee.

Poor managers are not looking to change and adapt in order to improve their own performance and believe that it is others who need to change rather than them.

Often, a dictatorial manager will be so because he or she has to hide behind the cloak of authority in order to protect self-esteem.

In coping with such a person you need to adapt to the manager's real needs for recognition and respect in order to create the change of stance necessary to win.

Development of ideas and strategies for an organization or group

Situation

Can you imagine what would happen if you were to ask different members of a management board to describe in fewer than 10 words what their business is and what is good about it? The likelihood is that, unless they have all been through a rigorous strategy development process, you would get a variety of different answers and likely disagreement on whose version is best.

This is because the operational management of the business and not strategy is their main, day-to-day preoccupation. They discharge what they would see as functional responsibilities perfectly well, and control finances, but visit strategic issues only rarely. To realize fully the potential of an organization or group requires a process that puts strategy, rather than just financial considerations, at the centre of the business and maximizes the likelihood of further growth and success.

If you, as a business leader, know where you want to be in, say, four to five years' time, you will automatically know where you want to be in one year's time. This means that it is possible to work out now what must be done to get there.

If, however, goals are not clearly defined, then planning cannot take place. Although it may be relatively easy to project financial figures, numbers alone can never fully represent strategy.

The strategic development process is, in fact, relatively straightforward. What is not so easy is to decide the strategy that drives the right changes in order to accelerate development.

By being clear about an organization's 'core competencies', that is to say those two or three key attributes that set it apart from others, together with the customers or stakeholders to which they apply, it will be possible to position the organization in the eyes of its public. This makes it much easier to decide business and operational priorities.

Behaviour

To develop strategy successfully requires a management team to be aligned behind a single purpose. This means considering all the options that are desirable or have a chance of being made to work and, initially at least, ruling nothing out.

It is often the case in management teams that they will include sceptics among their number. This is, in fact, a good thing as it challenges the status quo as well as stretching the resourcefulness of the leader or facilitator. Developing a strategy rarely means doing the same as you have always done and is primarily about creating a focus on which to concentrate the combined energy of the organization's resources.

The team will be successful if it works through the options, decision criteria and priorities to formulate a strategy based on key strengths, robust logic and shared beliefs.

It can often be the sceptics, through asking the most challenging questions, who create the realistic view that makes it easier for decisions to be made – however much they had resisted taking part in the strategy development process in the first place!

NLP observation

An important tenet of NLP is that to improve anything you first need to know the outcome you want. This is why the alignment of management teams behind a single vision is so important. Following this, you need to achieve common agreement about what needs to be done to achieve the vision. The strategic options usually cause differences of opinion, which is why you will need to try different approaches and behaviours until you get the result you want. Although members of the team believe they are talking about the same thing, their perspectives and reactions are inevitably different, so the role of the leader is to establish the common ground on which the process can move forward.

Having achieved the desired alignment and the who, what, where and when of the plan, NLP thinking says that you should immediately get on and do it.

If you always do what you always did, you will always get what you always got. In order to change something you need to change something in yourself as well as in your colleagues.

Getting the best from meetings

Situation

A meeting should be a dynamic device that enables the work of an organization to move forward efficiently, and to monitor and record that progress. People sometimes complain that they spend so much time in meetings that they cannot get their work done. The reality is that many meetings, because they are insufficiently prepared, take longer than necessary and do not move things forward to the extent they could.

Also, because meetings can contain such a variety of personalities, there is ample scope for differently motivated individuals to display a range of behaviours, including the tendency to dominate, under-contribute, go off on a tangent, obstruct progress or distort others' intentions.

The purpose of a meeting is to use the collaboration of minds in order to share information, check progress, identify issues, reach agreements, make good-quality decisions and plan activities.

More than 80 per cent of a meeting should be managed before and after it takes place. Its objectives should be clear as well as the specific outcomes that are required. This makes the best use of time, people and information. There is a strong dependency on both the meeting administrator and the person who chairs it to ensure that the meeting contributes effectively to the business of the organization.

Behaviour

Behaviour in meetings has, for fun, been characterized in the form of different animals and you will no doubt recognize some of their traits in people that you know.

Someone who is aggressive, inflexible and likely to attack when provoked could be a pit bull terrier. An intelligent person who is keen but rather boring and has a tendency to plod along could be a horse. Crafty people who have a tendency to undermine others are foxes, and know-it-alls who interrupt, question unnecessarily and constantly chatter could be considered monkeys. Then there are prickly hedgehogs, blabbermouth frogs and timid deer, all of whose contributions must be managed wisely.

It may be that the chair has deficiencies in managing others' contributions, permits distractions and allows time slippage. The minute taker may be at a loss about what to and what not to record, and minutes, instead of being produced and distributed within 24 hours while memories are still fresh, are written up just before the next meeting.

When a meeting has been well managed and outcomes are clear and agreed, it is highly motivational to the participants and gives confidence to others about the work of that organization or group.

NLP observation

Even those who sit in meetings but do not participate are communicating. Others will interpret silence or non-involvement as having an intention, and not that the person is entirely switched off. The challenge for the chair is to sense what might lie behind the silence and to create a situation where that person can be drawn in, for instance asking for a show of hands and then following up with a (leading) question as to why that person had or had not voted. It is also important to respect that every behaviour is appropriate in some context and to suspend judgement until some alignment has taken place.

A common issue in meetings is when people want to place blame, but NLP rejects the concept of failure, preferring to regard every potential instance as positive feedback. It is the equivalent of a company that welcomes customer complaints, without which it is robbed of an opportunity for continuous improvement.

Another NLP belief is that a person's behaviour is not who he or she is. This means regarding behaviour as a transitory rather than a permanent characteristic, and not reacting simply to that behaviour in some way but to the intention behind it.

A key skill of the chair is to establish and maintain rapport. No one is perfect but a harmonious team of diverse characters can be.

Meetings, in the same way as people or organizations, have to have a purpose and a tangible outcome. If you do not know what was intended, how do you know whether the meeting has been a success?

Managing teams and projects

Situation

If you are managing a project, whether it is in information technology (IT), construction, research, business development, or any other, you will be fully aware of the challenges and complexities involved in marshalling resources and ensuring that the right people do the right things in the right places at the right time. Projects have an infinite capacity for going wrong, which is why the role of project manager demands such a wide skill set, including the ability to listen, make decisions, communicate concisely and motivate others.

Assuming that a project was properly set up in the first place (and many are not), most go wrong because of inadequate communication between the project sponsor, the project implementation group and among the project teams. Communication in this context is a fundamental quality issue.

A common outcome of project mistakes is people's desire to allocate blame, when the reality is that both sides were involved in putting the project plan together in the first place.

One of the common occurrences in projects is that, as is their prerogative, people change their minds about a specification they had previously agreed. The way an ensuing change process is managed is critical to its success.

CASE STUDY

In a school building project, although designs and drawings may have been signed off, the placing of entrances and corridors can sometimes be changed because of some afterthought about, for example, rapid access for pupils in bad weather. The implications of making these adjustments extend far beyond mere structural change and will involve architects, surveyors, suppliers, workforce managers and many others, and add disproportionately to project costs and timescales. If changes have been allowed for in initial project planning, then change control procedures will be in place. If they have not been allowed for, then all change is disruptive.

Behaviour

Project sponsors usually know what they want in high-level terms but expect project management teams to deliver on the detail. The challenge for the project team, and in particular the manager of that team, is to interpret the sponsor's requirements and convert them to a specification that both parties agree to. The behavioural demands on the project team at that stage will be to ask a sufficient number of good questions in a constructive way so as to be able to execute the project to a precise, unambiguous brief.

Some of these questions may seem onerous to the sponsor, whose main wish is that they should 'get on with it' and use their own initiative, expertise or whatever is needed to ensure the project's success. The project team may become frustrated that the parties are communicating on a different level, which no doubt they are.

The project manager wants his or her team to understand the outcome of the project, the means of achieving it, to be flexible to changing demands and to deliver on time. This has to be communicated at the outset together with a continuous flow of communication for the duration of the project. The quality of written communication together with the precision and factual basis of verbal interchanges are essential attributes in ensuring well-coordinated team performance.

NLP observation

In projects it is important to realize that there will be different perspectives on the same thing and that a process of alignment has to take place. This requires an understanding of the mindsets of others, the way information is taken on board, and good use of verbal, visual and sensory stimuli in the process of communication.

In order to get round situations, you may need to modify your own behaviour until a result is achieved. Through modifying your own behaviour it is easier to get others to modify theirs.

To achieve the best from your team you will know that, if empowered, they have all the resources they need to ensure a successful outcome. Your own experience gives you understanding and therefore the capacity to explain something well to others, to motivate their actions, recognize their performance and help resolve any issues they may have.

If you are running a project on someone's behalf, recognizing any hidden agendas, preferences and prejudices is an essential part of the preparation. Your own assessment of their language, physical signals and patterns will help you to maintain the empathy and rapport that oils the wheels of the project.

In the case of dispute between yourself and the sponsor, or with or between team members, shifting the agenda on to facts and away from feelings (although you have to acknowledge these first) creates the only platform on which a satisfactory outcome can be achieved.

Managing others' motivation

Situation

Motivation matters. Why? Because there is ample proof that people who are happy in their work will perform better than those who are not. In terms of both productivity and quality of action, maximizing positive motivational feeling will assist performance. Conversely, where motivation is lacking, this will result in reduced performance and output, unhappy workers, increased absences due to stress or illness and frequent staff changes.

In situations where there are multiple effects (lots of staff) whether positive or negative motivation occurs, the result can impact hugely on any organization. If you are in charge of a department, running a business or working with teams or on projects, using NLP skills to increase positive motivation will bring great rewards.

Good motivation ensures that staff are as self-sufficient as possible. They feel empowered to take decisions and to work on their own, without recourse to line managers. The essential difference between motivated staff and demotivated staff is easily recognizable. People may be able to do something and do it satisfactorily if directed. Those who are willing to do it, able to do it and do it well are positively motivated, and their performance will be optimized.

> Good motivation ensures that staff are as self-sufficient as possible

Managers need to be able to motivate people, not leave them to work things out for themselves. Quite often in the workplace there are more examples of bad management than good. This is probably because positive motivation rarely just happens. It is an active process that needs to be worked at on a continuing basis. NLP believes that with experience comes understanding; only then can you explain something well. If you can explain something well, you will be able to motivate people to achieve great results. You will in effect be 'making it real' for those you are seeking to motivate.

Motivation is the opposite of management by fear. Only if people want to do things, and are encouraged to do things well, can they be relied on actually to do them really well. Motivation provides reasons for people to want to deliver good performance.

Behaviour

The first of the classic motivational theories that is worthy of note was documented by Douglas McGregor. He defined human behaviour relevant to organizational life as:

- Theory X: assumes that people are lazy, uninterested in work or responsibility and must be pushed or bribed to get anything done in a disciplined way, with a reward assisting the process.

- Theory Y: assumes the opposite view: people want to work, they enjoy a sense of achievement, gaining satisfaction from a job well done and assuming responsibility for it. They naturally seek ways of making work a positive experience.

These are of course extreme positions but there is truth in both pictures. If you have a job that is boring and mundane, it is not difficult to understand why it is hard to stay motivated. However, if your work is more interesting it is much easier to be motivated. In the former case, if you are a member of staff with a mundane repetitive job, your manager will need strong motivational skills to encourage you to work well.

Where motivation is concerned, NLP beliefs and assumptions can be applied in a number of ways. People respond according to their internal maps of reality and two people will see the same thing in entirely different ways. There is an apocryphal story about a despondent group of convicts breaking rocks being asked to express their feelings about the work. All of them expressed negative feelings, except one. He said: 'It makes it bearable if I keep the end result in mind – I'm helping to build a cathedral.'

Whether you believe that people fall mainly into the X or Y category, it is undeniable that motivation creates a process that draws the best from any situation. Good motivation can help people move from a Theory X position to a Theory Y one (even if they have a boring task to do). Motivation can reinforce a Theory Y position so that even better performance can be achieved, and so on.

NLP observation

Employees who lack motivation do not perform as well as their more motivated colleagues. Dissatisfiers (factors that lead people to switch off) can include: company policy and administrative processes; supervision (micro-management); working conditions; salary; relationship with co-workers; status and security. All of these factors (demotivators) contain considerable potential for diluting any positive motivational feeling.

The satisfiers (motivators) that create positive motivation include: achievement; recognition; work itself; responsibility; advancement and growth. These factors, when used by managers, will ensure that people want to perform well. Communication is a vital part of this. Every piece of communication has motivational repercussions. Consider another appropriate NLP belief: it is impossible not to communicate. The important thing where motivation is concerned is to communicate effectively so as to produce an enhanced result.

In terms of NLP beliefs and assumptions, the meaning of your communication is the response that you get. Say a system at your workplace has been upgraded. Instead of the old method, it is now essential that staff fill in a new form after completing a certain process on a regular basis. If it is not made clear why this is necessary, people will be demotivated. They may even go so far as to forget to complete the required documentation, or fill it in inaccurately after the event.

If you are to be a good motivator, it is essential that as supervisor, you explain exactly why the new form needs to be completed. Once employees understand the significance and purpose of the new process, they are far more likely to take 'ownership' of it and carry out the instructions willingly, responsibly and accurately.

NLP believes that with experience comes understanding; only then can you explain something well. When attempting to influence the motivational climate, it is important to include understanding as well as instruction in your dealings with staff. Should you be new to management, or tasked with leading a project team for the first time, the following motivation techniques should prove helpful:

- Job descriptions, clear guidelines and adequate training – all these give staff a feeling of security. Without these motivation suffers.

- Incentives – these work less effectively if their details are not clearly communicated. If an incentive payment scheme is so complicated that no one understands it, staff will not be able to work out how they are doing. Motivation will decrease as a result despite the terms of the deal being generous. Management will then be resentful and a vicious circle will arise.

- Routine jobs – these can be made much more bearable by communicating to people what an important contribution they are making to the organization as a whole. This is a common problem. If you can work on this, your department will be much more productive and staff morale will improve.

- Job titles – what's in a name? If job titles are sensibly chosen with a view to how they affect people's feelings of status, as well as acting as a description of function, this is positively motivating. Your job may be described as 'sales executive' but this could mean many things. An enlightened manager would understand your request for a change of description to an 'account service manager'.

- Recognition – perhaps the simplest and least expensive positive motivational act someone can perform is to say 'Well done' to a member of staff. If it can be done in public, or in print, the effect is multiplied many times over. In NLP terms, modifying your own behaviour can make others change. If you don't take the time to say thank you to staff for a job well done, try doing so in future. The result could be far greater than you imagined.

Managing time in others

Situation

You may have the unenviable task of trying to increase the output of your staff. Your company may be on a drive to deliver results faster and more effectively. How can you get people to work more productively? You can see that they are busy all of the day but what are they actually doing? Why do hours pass with much activity but sometimes precious little achievement? Are they aware that working efficiently is not enough?

> Many people make the mistake of measuring activity when they should be measuring the outcome

To get the most out of their time they should be working effectively. Many people make the mistake of measuring activity when they should be measuring the outcome. In the context of time management, being busy should not be confused with output. Good time management means working out what action produces the best result.

Behaviour

Urgent/important

Do your staff put off doing things that should really be done straight away? Quite often something that is urgent can be done quickly. If you got to your place of work and found there was water pouring out of the kitchen, what would you do? It wouldn't take long to shut off the mains water supply. It might take longer to mop up the wet floor, but hopefully that wouldn't be your job. It would only take a few seconds to turn the stopcock and deal with the crisis. Help your staff to define what urgent tasks are. Encourage them to get these out of the way as quickly as possible so that they don't waste any more time in their working day.

Being perfect

Some people overdo things – particularly things they like. This is an easy trap to fall into where time management is concerned. Watch out that staff do not spend far longer than they need doing something simply because they enjoy it. You know (and they know) there is a less pleasant task waiting to be tackled. Limit the amount of time you give someone to hand in a piece of work. If you issue jobs with short deadlines, it prevents staff from continually perfecting something, so as to avoid starting tasks they are reluctant to begin.

Lists

If staff are having difficulty achieving results, issue them with agendas or 'to do' lists. A short meeting at the beginning of the day could set out what needs to be finished by the end of the week. Certain tasks should be 'A' list items; these should be urgent and important. Less urgent or important tasks should be 'B' list items. If you are distributing tasks throughout a department or project team, make sure you are aware of individuals' strengths. It is far easier to achieve a good result if you filter jobs to complement these. Do not ask someone who has difficulty writing reports to prepare the minutes of the recent meeting. Always give praise when work is handed in on time. This will encourage others to work effectively in future.

Minimize interruptions

There is no doubt that in the workplace random interruptions can eat up hours of productive work time. Do not allow people to wander off with papers in their hand with a vague excuse of 'Just going to a meeting.' Be specific: ask what meeting, with whom, how long will you be? Check that people are working, not just scanning the internet for their next holiday destination. Keep an eye on how long people spend on the telephone or whether they are constantly sending or replying to e-mails that are unnecessary. Technology has made it far easier to waste time than ever before because there is so much choice of how to communicate.

Be selective

One good tip for achieving good time management is to do one thing at a time. Some staff pride themselves on being multi-taskers. This probably means they do lots of things – not particularly well. Or there are lots of half-completed projects on the go at any given time. Discuss with them what is most important, ask them to complete it and bring it to you. Then encourage them to move on to the next thing. There is nothing more satisfying than closure. Once they get the hang of this, they will find their effectiveness increases.

NLP observation

When applying NLP beliefs and assumptions in the context of time management, it is important to remember that people are not their words and behaviour. Staff may feel they are doing their best by being busy and being active. But if they are not doing the right things, activity alone achieves little if anything. They are not wrong to be fully occupied, but neither are they right in the sense of good time management.

A positive intention motivates every behaviour. Someone is late delivering a piece of work, because they want you to have a perfectly executed document. The deadline is missed, you do not have the paper you need at the time you want it and have to improvise. The member of staff did not intend to cause trouble, but unwittingly did so. Make instructions clear next time. Don't think 'failure', think 'opportunity to learn' for both of you.

Another NLP belief is that two people will see the same thing in entirely different ways. When trying to improve time management it is important that staff are able to prioritize, and to distinguish an urgent from an important task. Rarely will two people be looking at things from the same standpoint. You will be disappointed by their failure to achieve output unless you spend time identifying with them what is a priority task (to them, to you, to the organization) and what can be done later.

> Rarely will two people be looking at things from the same standpoint

Cinderella and behavioural traits in organizations

The story of Cinderella provides a useful allegory to situations that are often encountered in business. Anyone who has read the story as a child will quickly recognize parallels to specific individuals from everyday life.

Situation

The team of characters in the story could be described in a cast list as follows:

- Cinderella – a deliberately repressed employee.
- Ugly Sisters – bullying 'managers' or supervisors.
- Cinderella's father – weak, somewhat disinterested leader.
- Cinderella's stepmother – selfish and manipulative Headquarters (HQ) manager.
- Fairy Godmother – external human resources (HR) consultant.
- The Prince – an eager customer.

Cinderella's situation is that she is continuously bombarded with tasks by the Ugly Sisters, deliberately denied development and growth, and has no involvement in deciding what she does and when she does it. There is no interest provided by the work, no colleagues to confer with and no challenges to stimulate her mind and her imagination.

The Ugly Sisters are in the position they are more because of circumstance than ability. They assume that they know how to manage Cinderella, probably through copying what they think other managers do.

Cinderella's father feels unable to stand up to his new partner and those she has introduced into 'the firm'. He would prefer a quiet life to confrontation. Cinderella's stepmother wants to exercise control without necessarily contributing to the business or improving the circumstances of the workers.

The Fairy Godmother, a consultant who has been a friend of the firm for some time, can see what is going on but has no direct influence on the management team so has to think of other strategies to improve Cinderella's status and well-being. She has just been studying the operational principles of NLP!

The Prince is simply looking for an attractive, trouble-free outcome to ensure the long-term continuity of his family enterprise.

Behaviour

Until the external consultant comes along, Cinderella has no choice but to comply with the wishes of the Ugly Sisters. They, in turn, have no incentive or guidance to behave differently, and besides, their prejudiced mother supports their interests to the exclusion of all else. By doing nothing, the father condones behaviour that he might otherwise criticize if he were stronger.

The Fairy Godmother establishes a strong rapport with Cinderella preparatory to convincing her to do something she would otherwise have regarded as impossible. Subject to certain caveats, she accepts the challenge.

The Prince behaves like a prince because that is his duty, but allows himself to be unduly influenced by his emotions. In these circumstances, that proves to be a good thing and ultimately leads to the desired outcome.

NLP observation

The Ugly Sisters saw Cinderella as a 'problem to be fixed' rather than an opportunity to develop new contacts, which in reality it was. The negative approach made it that much harder to realize a positive outcome. Cinderella had no enthusiasm until she was given a vision of what was possible. Through establishing rapport with her, the Fairy Godmother was then able to lead her thoughts in a positive direction.

The stepmother's view of the world was limited by her own short-term perspective and irrational support for her daughters.

By doing what she always did, she was unlikely to uncover a new way of doing things.

The Fairy Godmother changed her own and others' perspectives in order to achieve something that others would have said was impossible. NLP says that we all have all the resources that we need to do anything we want. The Prince faithfully followed NLP operating principles.

Below are real-life quotes from real managers (with negative dispositions) who might now wish that they had written something different:

> We could have a brief chat tomorrow provided that there is something time-critical, which I do not feel there is.

> Will you ensure that, when bringing problems to the meeting, you also propose a solution. Problems without solutions will not be discussed at the meeting.

> XYZ [entrepreneur] has a will to win like no other I have seen but also a lack of experience and know-how that is currently a disadvantage.

Chapter 11
Opportunities for personal development

Assertiveness in challenging situations

Situation

No doubt at some point you will have dealings with difficult people. Some can be awkward, some troublesome, some downright horrendous. It pays to use NLP skills to cope appropriately with unmanageable characters so as to get the best out of the situation (for both sides). One company director described his knack of successfully handling challenging situations as having the combined skills of an acrobat, a diplomat and a doormat – flexibility, a smooth tongue and knowing when to back down. The solution, he believed, was correctly assessing in which order and in what proportion to implement them all.

But what really matters is your ability to be assertive. When faced with a challenging situation this is essential. You will gain nothing by being aggressive, or passive. Assertiveness is a skill that can be learned. If you deal with a challenging situation in an assertive way, the result is that you leave it feeling OK about yourself and the other person involved does as well. You may also achieve a win–win outcome, which would have the benefit of mutual respect and self-respect. The ideal solution is to have no anxiety about the circumstances afterwards, or to harbour any guilt, resentment, embarrassment or frustration.

Behaviour

The difference between being aggressive, passive and assertive can be clarified in this way:

- An aggressive response is a put-down. It could be a personal attack, tinged with sarcasm and arrogance.

- A passive response is your choice not to say or do anything confrontational. But it can leave you feeling frustrated afterwards.

- An assertive response is a reasonable objection which is delivered in a polite yet positive manner.

So if you get nothing out of passive behaviour and you can lose a good deal from behaving aggressively, what's it worth to be assertive? The gain is that you feel good about yourself and the other person. The bonus is the lack of anxiety and guilt. Once you have worked out and understood what the tangible benefits are, it will make it easier for you to behave in a more assertive way in future. Here are three sample situations.

Scenario 1: imagine you've been asked to work over the weekend for the second time this month. You know the importance of the deadline, but you've had some other plans in place for a long time which involve other people. These could be a significant family celebration where your absence would mar the occasion. What do you do?

You could simply refuse to come in to work, saying you've already done your fair share since you worked the previous weekend. You might even say it's time they picked on someone else.

Or you could resign yourself to the fact that working over the weekend is inevitable and it's just another example of work coming before everything else. This upsets your family and leaves you feeling resentful and guilty the whole time.

You could say you have other commitments but, if it would be useful, you'll come in early on the Monday morning and stay late a couple of evenings to help complete the project on time. Which do you think is the assertive response and which answer would you be likely to choose?

Scenario 2: in a meeting, a colleague presents one of your ideas as her own. How would you react?

Perhaps you say nothing, because you're worried about causing an argument in front of everyone else. But you might have a word with her afterwards to set the record straight. You express disbelief and firmly point out that this was your idea in the first place. You say you resent the fact that she's been underhand in trying to gain the credit for something of which she can't claim ownership.

What about this: say how pleased you are that she's backing your idea and invite her to collaborate with you on the project. This defuses the situation completely and disarms your opponent. She can hardly be angry when you are giving praise in front of other people in recognition of her supporting your idea.

Scenario 3: you have an urgent piece of work to complete so you ask your assistant to help you. He says he has an even more important task to finish for another person so he can't help.

Do you try to bribe him to fit your work in, but realize that you'll probably end up doing it yourself anyway? Or try pulling rank and say there's no way your deadline can be missed and the other person's work can't be as important? You insist he stays late to finish your project.

Or you could explain about the urgency: that the work has to be finished today. But you offer to negotiate on his behalf with the other colleague, so that there is no misunderstanding about why their piece of work is being laid aside to help you.

NLP observation

When trying to deal with challenging situations assertively, NLP beliefs can be applied in several ways. If you are a normally passive person, and you do what you always do, you will get what you've always got. In other words, if you're a natural doormat, you will continually be put upon and you will feel increasing resentment and frustration each time it happens. If you tend to be aggressive when faced with a challenge you may get angry with people when they ask you to do something. But if this is your usual manner, they will expect this from you and take no notice. You may still be expected to work late despite your anger and bad feeling.

NLP also states that people have all the resources they need: it is just a question of applying them. You have the ability to deal assertively in challenging situations, but you need to equip yourself with the skills and practise them until they become your normal response.

The most common reasons for not dealing assertively when faced with a difficult set of circumstances are: fear of being ignored, fear of humiliation and fear of being rejected.

Try this: first acknowledge that there is a problem. Someone wants you to do something and you either cannot or do not wish to agree to their wishes. You need to keep a check on your emotional responses, your body language and your thought processes. Do not react instantly. Take some thinking time. NLP states that success depends on varying what you do until you get the result that you want. Don't automatically agree to someone's unreasonable request. Don't lash out in an angry outburst and then regret what you've just said. Take time to rationalize and then communicate carefully, clearly and positively. (If it's a really sensitive or tricky matter try to enlist support or advice from a colleague or superior.) NLP states that the meaning of your communication is the response that you get.

If you can be flexible in your approach and review your ideal outcome – what really would be the best solution for you and for them and what you are realistically likely to achieve – you should be successful. Remember, NLP also states that modifying your own behaviour can make others change.

> Remember, NLP also states that modifying your own behaviour can make others change

Do make sure you have analysed the problem. In other words, differentiate between facts ('These dates/figures are incorrect'), assumptions ('This report must have been prepared by an idiot member of staff'), generalities ('You never check your information for accuracy') and emotions ('How can I possibly trust you when you do this?'). NLP beliefs state that people respond accordingly to their internal maps of reality. Be certain of what your map is telling you.

Confidence in your own abilities

Situation

Confidence in your own ability is something that everyone needs. Most people have it, though at times they may not believe it. If you are confident, the most important thing is to ensure that your body language does not convey a different impression. An important NLP belief is that it is you who has control of your mind and therefore the results that you achieve.

Self-confidence varies from person to person in different situations. You may be supremely confident of your abilities in certain circumstances yet in other situations you may feel nervous or ill at ease. No one is the same and each individual's ability to show confidence is entirely personal. If you sometimes lack confidence in your own abilities, one way of changing that is to learn confidence-building skills. This requires preparation and a bit of practice. It also needs to be actively worked at to ensure you create the right impression at the appropriate time.

You may be extremely talented as an economist, clever at interpreting figures and produce excellent charts and graphs to express future business trends. These skills are invaluable to your organization. However, if your self-confidence is low and your presentation skills are weak, no one will believe what your predictions show. This could have a detrimental effect, not only on you when you're delivering the information, but also on the audience, who will not be engaged with your communication. Finally it will reflect adversely on your organization, on whose behalf you are presenting your facts.

If you know you are good at something, then you should be able to carry things off with confidence. But sometimes it isn't all that easy to appear confident in situations at work. Although you have the right answers, circumstances – other people, or technology – can conspire against you. So having a few basic confidence-building skills at your fingertips will help. You won't come across in a confident way by trickery or by faking it. This is a false premise – people will see through it or (worse) you will trip yourself up. To be businesslike and professional you need a step-by-step approach.

Behaviour

Do you notice when colleagues are nervous? Do you work with people who have low self-esteem? Is this because they are not able to perform tasks well and are afraid of being seen as under-performing? Or are they more than up to their job but simply shy in certain circumstances? If you meet someone who is fidgeting, tightly clasping and unclasping their hands, keeping their head bowed or avoiding eye contact, they may be suffering acute lack of confidence despite having ability in their specific area. Some people who are nervous cross their arms or hold their papers or briefcase in front of them. Anything like this displays a form of self-protection.

The more confident you are, the more likely you'll exhibit relaxed gestures and open body language. You will give the impression of being able to take whatever comes your way 'full frontal'. If you are an extrovert personality, you may use your arms to gesticulate – open movements indicate a confident personality. The less you move your limbs and the closer they are kept to your body, the more you'll indicate that you're a shy or timid person.

The best way to be seen as a confident and self-assured individual who exudes a cool, professional manner is to use open body language. People who stand upright, balanced on both feet with weight evenly distributed and arms relaxed at their side, are in control. Don't forget that the body is an instrument. It conveys emotion. Other people can pick up on these signals easily and they will react more positively to confident gestures. A greatly reassuring sign is when someone mirrors your body language. By copying what the other person does, it endorses the favourable (if that is what they are showing) view they have formed of you. If you reinforce a positive impression, you create a bond between yourself and the other party.

> Don't forget that the body is an instrument

When you are trying to create a favourable impression with someone, your body will quite naturally point towards them. This can be unconscious but will be noticed by the other person. If you have the opportunity, have a look at how individuals position themselves when communicating with each other. Most people usually angle themselves towards the person with whom they wish to create a positive impression. They turn away from those whom they seek to avoid. Maintaining good eye contact is an important factor. Keep your eyes directed towards the other person at all times but avoid an unblinking stare – this can be unnerving.

NLP observation

In order to improve your confidence whether generally or, specifically, in your own abilities, spend a little time asking colleagues or friends whom you trust what they notice about you. In NLP people are not their words and behaviour. But it is also impossible not to communicate. You do not want to communicate a lack of confidence – yet many people do not realize when they are doing just that. A little 360° feedback is very helpful here.

Are you regarded as a confident person? What are the situations and occasions where you lack confidence? What kind of image do you currently present? Do you usually make a favourable impression on people at a first meeting? How do people react when meeting you? How would you like people to respond to you?

It is essential to develop a positive mental attitude. People rarely take longer than a few seconds to make a judgement about someone. So if your presentation skills aren't strong, spend a little time and effort on your appearance to give your confidence a boost. One of NLP's main principles asks: is it better to judge your intentions or your actions? Remember that the outcome of many situations is often determined by the confidence shown by the parties involved.

Once you have begun to exude confidence in yourself and your abilities, it will get easier to extend the boundaries. Confidence is like a muscle – it grows stronger as you exercise it.

> Confidence is like a muscle – it grows stronger as you exercise it

Communicating verbally with others one to one

Situation

You are about to have an important first meeting with someone. The outcome could be significant for you personally, your career or your organization. Your communication skills are being put to the test. Face-to-face meetings can be daunting and sometimes awkward for those not brimming with confidence and experience. The most important thing to work out beforehand is: what message do you wish to get across? In other words, what are you trying to achieve during the dialogue? You must be certain of two things: what information you wish to convey and what you want the other person to do as a result.

In one-to-one communication, clarity is paramount. Communication is signalling: transmission by the speaker of a message that should evoke understanding in the receiver. This sounds straightforward enough, but it can be fraught with danger – in practice things can, and often do, go wrong. In business relationships particularly there are plenty of opportunities for misunderstanding and ambiguity.

In presentation skills, if only 7 per cent of the impact you make comes from the words you speak (the remainder is visual – appearance, sound of voice and body language) it is vital that your words come across well. What you say can be broken down into three parts: the type of words you use, the sort of sentences and how you phrase them.

To communicate effectively on a one-to-one basis, consider the words, the ideas and the structure of the message you wish to convey. Keep it as simple as possible. Always aim for clarity over ambiguity. Commonly used words, in short direct sentences, have the greatest impact. They also allow the least margin for error or misinterpretation.

Behaviour

In face-to-face encounters the key to success is to get on the other person's wavelength as soon as possible. By demonstrating empathy with them you will find the communication between each of you is much smoother and more positive. Be sure to demonstrate your listening skills. This means relying on the 2 : 1 ratio – using your ears twice as much as your mouth. Many people are poor listeners. There is nothing more damaging to one-to-one communication than being involved in a one-sided conversation. This is where one party is interested only in the sound of their own voice.

Good listening avoids misunderstandings. Someone who listens attentively keeps a comfortable level of eye contact and has an open and relaxed but alert pose. You should face the speaker and respond to what is being said with appropriate facial expressions. You can acknowledge what is being said and offer encouragement with a nod or a smile.

> Good listening avoids misunderstandings

One useful tip is using the reflecting and summarizing method. Repeat back a key word or phrase the speaker has used. This demonstrates that you have listened and understood. Summarizing gives the speaker the chance to add or amend your understanding if needed.

Successful face-to-face communication requires a balance of listening and talking. Should you wish to find out a lot of information, avoid the trap of asking too many questions. No one wants a 'Spanish Inquisition'. Only one person at a time can truly direct a conversation. One person leads and the other follows. If there is to be an opening ritual (small talk about some general topic) watch for the moment when this should cease and the meeting begin. If there seems to be no plan, someone should take the lead – and the best person to do this is you.

The early part of any meeting is a key stage for your confidence. You'll feel and operate better if you get off to a planned start. You'll also be able to maintain better control and direct the rest of the exchange. Good conversational techniques involve a balanced style

> The early part of any meeting is a key stage for your confidence

of communication. You could begin the exchange by introducing yourself and giving some personal information. This is called the *inform* stage. Once you've done this, ask a direct question of the other party. This is called the *invite* stage. Then *wait* for their response. When it is given, *listen* well. Then *acknowledge* and – if necessary – *repeat* the essence of their response.

If you can achieve this cycle of communication, it can be repeated many times over during a conversation to establish good rapport between both parties. This formula works as well in business communication as it does in a social context.

NLP observation

Communicating verbally on a one-to-one basis is an essential skill. In NLP assumptions, it is impossible not to communicate. But it is very difficult to communicate effectively and positively unless you adhere to these basic communication rules:

- Presence: pay attention to the way your voice and body language are used in conjunction with the words you speak. They should be congruent. You will convey a positive impression if they are used correctly. An NLP assumption states that context is what determines others' interpretation of any action or communication.

- Relating: it is essential to develop rapport with the other party as early as possible – empathize with them. In NLP, mind and body are different expressions of the same system. The way someone thinks will affect how they feel. If you want a successful one-to-one meeting with someone, be empathetic towards the other person.

- Questioning: when engaged in dialogue, make sure your questions are pertinent to the situation or subject. Anything irrelevant will betray that you've not been paying attention to what was said. Remember, in NLP it is you who has control of your mind and therefore the results that you achieve.

- Checking: while engaged in dialogue, keep good eye contact with the other person to see that they are still on your wavelength. Watch for the gestures they make, are they positive or negative? When they are talking, what signals are you giving in response? The meaning of your communication is the response that you get.

Managing your time

Situation

In terms of time management is it really important to do more? Should every second of every minute be filled with work? Results by volume are fine in some cases, but where personal time management is concerned, often *less* is *more*. Does this make any sense? Surely you need to be productive and that means working harder and faster? Not necessarily. Perhaps your time management could be improved if you are aware that time passes and some days not a huge amount is achieved. Maybe doing what you've always done, you'll get what you've always got. And doing it that bit faster won't help much either.

One way to manage time is to actively work at doing nothing for a certain amount of time each day. Build in some thinking time and cut down on being quite so busy. Why is this important? Because if you don't have time to think creatively or 'out of the box', you will never get around to doing those really important jobs that just aren't getting done. These are the things that can change your life. The way to accomplish more is by doing less.

Behaviour

Elimination

What do you have to do today? Is your list endless? Maybe one way to go about this is to write out the things you want to do – make two columns 'A' and 'B'. The A list tasks are the more important. The B lists tasks can wait till tomorrow. Then tear the list in half and throw away the B list. Start again, and divide the A list into two columns. Decide which are the more important items and put them in the first column and the less important in the second column. Repeat the process – throw away the B list. By now you should have some idea of what's going on. If you need to, do it again. You are likely to end up with between three and six tasks on your list which *really* matter. Get on with those – now – and leave the rest.

Effectiveness v efficiency

In essence, efficiency is performing a task (whether important or not) in the most economical manner possible. Effectiveness is doing things that get you closer to achieving your desired goals. If you don't know what these are, grab yourself some thinking time soon to work them out. It is important to realize that doing something unimportant well does not make it important. What you do is infinitely more important than how you do it. Don't be fooled into believing that thinking is tantamount to doing nothing. It is not. Thinking constructively is extremely hard work.

Self-analysis

When you are happy, you work more effectively. If you are working effectively, you achieve your goals. If this is not happening at the moment, you need to look at what is causing you problems or anxiety. What is it that has the opposite result – satisfaction and a feeling of achievement? These questions should be applied across the board in your work life: hours you work, type of work, location, colleagues, clients, customers, marketing and finances – even where you live. Should there be things that you can change, use your thinking time to work out how this could be done. Don't waste time attempting to change things that are unalterable. But if you are brave enough to step outside your straitjacket of routine activities, you will be able to make decisions that could change your life for ever. This will go far beyond improving your time management.

NLP observation

People respond according to their internal maps of reality. You may be conditioned to think that if you are busy you are managing your time well, being productive and achieving a lot. The opposite may in fact be the case. Unless you are working at important tasks, you are possibly wasting your time. Take time out to decide what you should be doing, and what you do well and effectively. No one can afford the time not to do this.

Success depends on varying the things you do until you get the result that you want. Are you better at working in the early hours of the day, rather than late at night? Can you produce more if you work in an interruption-free zone? Do you work best under pressure, or do you prefer a long-way-off deadline? Whatever it is you need to do to achieve greater satisfaction in your job and improved output, this should be worked at and adjusted until you achieve optimum results.

It is you who has control of your mind and therefore the results that you achieve. Unless you spend time thinking about what you are trying to do, you are wasting your own valuable personal resources. You could also be wasting the time of your staff, your superiors and your organization. You have the ability to change things, to influence others to your way of thinking. This can have far-reaching effects, way beyond that of time management, although that is where the process starts.

Managing your receptiveness to change

Situation

Change happens and you can do very little about it. You might try ignoring it, but does it go away? No. All you are doing effectively is putting on dark glasses so that you can't see exactly what is happening around you. You can try to stop it, but you won't succeed. Don't fool yourself into thinking you can stop progress. You might try insulating yourself from it for a while. If this helps you, fine. But it is only a temporary respite.

Change just keeps on happening. Like it or loathe it, you can't get away from it. Sometimes changes are for the better, other times change seems to makes things worse. Perhaps you feel you've had just about enough of it for the time being. When it happens, and it is set to affect you, there's not much you can do about it. To ignore change is dangerous. This is putting your organization and yourself at risk.

So many people in business try to fight change. It is pointless wasting your energy in this way. You are going to lose the battle and you will become a casualty of the conflict, rather than a survivor. The stress you feel in opposing the inevitable will make you ill. Luckily, NLP skills can help you overcome several aspects of dealing with change.

Behaviour

Change can bring excitement to your life, if you embrace it. But many people do not. There are four distinct phases that most people experience in response to it:

1 They deny it. When change occurs, the first response most people have is denial. Haven't you heard colleagues say 'That'll never work', 'What a stupid idea', 'If we wait a bit maybe they'll get back to the old way of doing things.' No organization can survive if it is staffed by ostriches. You may want to bury your head in the sand, believing if you can't see something it isn't there. But actually change is around you and it is not going away.

2 They become members of the resistance movement. If colleagues or staff are resistant to change, they won't accept it. They stick with the old way of doing things: 'If it was good enough in the past, there's no point in changing the way we operate.' You may feel you are right to say 'If it ain't broke, don't fix it.' But you will get stuck in a rut if you can't move forward. The sooner you become familiar with

the new system or process, the safer it is for your career and your organization. You will also keep your blood pressure from rising too high.

3 A bit of exploration takes place. After a while people realize that sticking to the old ways just isn't going to work. Tentatively they have a look to see if the new process has any advantages. If they find that it makes things a bit easier for them, perhaps it's worth having a go at using the new method. You may begin now to look at change with a more open mind. Although you are aware that some bad things have come from it, it isn't all bad and you begin to work on your strategy for managing the change.

4 Accepting change. This is the final phase of the process. You will find that you have successfully integrated the change into your way of working. It hasn't been the complete disaster you first thought it would be. You even admit that it's a lot better than the old way of doing things. The change is now the status quo and you have taken it on board and work with it not against it.

You will find that once this has happened, you have come full circle and the next time change is thrust upon you, you will not be so determined to resist it with all your energy.

Check whether you are resistant to change

Do you use old methods and processes when there are new rules you could incorporate into your work practices? Keep up to speed with technological advances and if you need further skills training, ask for it. No organization wants to drag its feet because its staff aren't capable of adapting quickly enough.

Are you afraid of taking on new challenges? If so, it is either because you are already overworked or because you're nervous about new situations and work methods. Don't be resistant to change because it could wipe out some of the tasks you perform or (worse) remove the need for your position altogether. Look positively at learning new skills and accept new assignments when they are offered.

Are you trying to slow the pace of change? However much you would like to embrace change, you feel you need time to adapt. Unfortunately new things usually mean an increase in speed, not a reduction in pace. Your organization needs to remain competitive in the marketplace, and it simply isn't economic to slow down every time something new comes along. Let technology take the strain – it is faster and you can do a lot more with a lot less if you allow this change to happen.

Are you using energy to control something that cannot be contained? This is such a waste. You can't stop growing older every year, nor can you stop night from following day. If you are attempting to resist change by trying to control things at work, you will not achieve anything. If the organization is undergoing radical changes, or there is a possibility of a merger or acquisition, there is nothing you can do about it. Either you continue to resist change and risk becoming ill through stress, or you lose your job because you cannot keep pace with new methods. Or you start learning how to respond to change and use it to help you progress.

Are you experiencing paralysis – frozen still and unable to move? This is the worst sign of resistance to change and is usually fatal. If change seems so overwhelming to you perhaps it's best to give up. You won't be able to perform your duties, because your resistance to change is so deep rooted. This situation nearly always ends in termination of employment. Don't allow this to happen.

NLP observation

Why not embrace change, and use the energy to leverage it to your advantage? People respond according to their internal maps of reality. You may need to redraw your map and become an admirer of progress rather than an opponent. If you always do what you always did, you will always get what you always got. Where adapting to change is concerned, you could find yourself burnt out and put out.

Being flexible and responsive to changes within your organization will set you on a strong upward path. People have all the resources they need; it is just a question of applying them. You could be an influence for good among those who continue to resist change. Become a shining example to others of how you made change work for you instead of against you.

Leaders of your organization will recognize that you have adapted to change and succeeded in incorporating new methods into your work practice. This will make it likely that you will be considered for promotion as part of the new order. Your organization will realize that your ability to embrace change rather than resist it makes you an incredibly valuable asset. With experience comes understanding; only then can you explain something well. You will be a survivor and your example, your responsiveness to change, will enable you to inspire others.

Chapter 12
Specific skills and capabilities to widen your range

Getting the best out of interviews

Situation

In the workplace, interviews are mostly associated with selecting a candidate or seeking a position for yourself. Either way, selection criteria will be based on skills, knowledge, qualifications, experience and, most importantly, a set of attitudes that creates sufficient rapport between the parties.

When interviewing others, you will be conscious that it is as easy to select the wrong candidate as to choose the right one, and that you may not find out whether you made the right choice until several weeks or months later. Beyond the glowing aspects of a curriculum vitae (CV) and a convincing presence, you will want to find the real person and to understand the contribution that they can genuinely make to your organization.

The fact that some people are good at being interviewed does not necessarily indicate that they will be good at the job. As an alternative to this, it may be worth considering a 'group assessment centre' approach where several candidates effectively compete for a position. This gives you as the employer the opportunity to observe objectively how different individuals cope with specific tasks and with each other, and then provides a basis for a much more direct and revealing one-on-one interview afterwards.

As an interviewer it can sometimes be difficult to balance the amount of information you should give with the amount of information you should receive from the candidate. With a reserved candidate it can be all too easy to compensate for that reserve with saying too much yourself and missing the responses against which you can make a reasonable assessment. How many times have you heard 'He only asked me three questions and talked himself for the rest of the time'?

Although it is true that interviews are a two-way sales process, it is the prerogative of the interviewer to control the process and modify his or her approach in order to reach the right basis for assessment.

When selling yourself as a candidate at an interview, it is easy to believe that talking about how good you are will endear you to the interviewer. Claiming that you will be an excellent employee who will excel in the interviewer's environment will be less convincing than being specific about the contribution you believe you could make and why. Generalization and abstract claims tend not to work in your favour.

Behaviour

If an interviewee says 'I'm really good at selling', that is less impressive than saying 'I've exceeded my sales targets for the last three years.' A claim without evidence to back it means very little. Likewise, if body language and tone imply arrogance, it will produce a non-neutral response in the interviewer, who will either resist that arrogance or, if of a compliant nature, will submit to it but probably switch off. Either way, it skews the interview and probably leads to an unsatisfactory result.

Conversely, if an interviewer says 'Right then, tell me what you can do for my department or our organization', the candidate has no clue about what, in the eyes of that interviewer, will put him or her in a good light and is likely to feel disadvantaged rather than encouraged. The reply may be less effective as a result and the interviewer will have learned little of value to the selection process.

Many interviewers are ill-prepared, may not have read a CV thoroughly or simply do not appreciate how to ask the questions that reveal the real person behind the factual information. As a result, the interview does not flow and it is a less than satisfactory learning process for both participants.

Interviewees may not have considered fully how to present themselves in the best light. It may be in the way they dress, the way they speak or the attitudes that they display. They have not taken account of the needs and wants of the interviewer and may just be seeing things through their own eyes. They are unlikely to be able to influence the interviewer if they do not really know what the interviewer wants.

NLP observation

Because two people will always see things in different ways, it is important for interviewer and interviewee to have considered the other's perspective in preparing for an interview. In the interview itself, adjustments always have to be made in order to ensure mutual understanding of the information exchanged. In a case where information is hard to extract, the approach will need to be varied until you get the result that you want.

Interviewer and interviewee need to be able to sense feelings, reactions, body language and the underlying meaning of the words used to convey questions and answers. Picking up the differences between generalized comments and observations, whether points have been accepted or deflected and contexts are clear or unambiguous are all part of the interviewer's and interviewee's necessary skills.

Writing reports

Situation

Have you ever been sent a report, started reading it with interest and then become frustrated by its sheer monotony and failure to retain your attention? Sadly, a high proportion of reports falls into this category.

One UK city council produces so many reports in one year that if each were read cover to cover, it would take someone over a year's full-time work to read every one. On this basis, if everyone who was supposed to read these reports did so thoroughly, then there would be no time for the other work for which they were being paid.

The upshot of too many over-lengthy reports is, of course, that they do not get read thoroughly, they do not communicate the full understanding that was intended and therefore cannot be fully effective.

If you were to ask someone what a report was about, you would probably be given a verbal precis that covered just a few key points. It is unlikely that you would be given a detailed account, but simply the highlights that made the biggest impact on the report's reader – assuming, of course, that they had read it thoroughly.

It may often be that key points are not made until after many pages of reading and may, as a consequence, be lost among the detail as compared to being highlighted early on. A good report will have 'navigation aids' and a structure that enables particular points or 'landmarks' to be identified more easily.

Of course, reports are produced in many different ways for many different purposes and can include journalistic reports, meeting minutes, inspection reviews, performance appraisals, monthly management reports, research feedback, accident records and so on. The common factor is that they are written (or spoken) for someone else and not for the author's own gratification.

Bearing this in mind, the overarching principle is that they should take account of the recipients' needs and wants in relation to the reported information. The starting point for any report is thus to consider the specific impact you want to achieve and the best way to 'get into the minds' of your audience.

Behaviour

Contrary to the writer's probable intention, most reports will not be read from beginning to end. The usual pattern of behaviour is to read the first few lines (to establish context) and to skim the document as a whole, looking for the most interesting bits. Some of the interesting bits may be read and many of the less interesting bits will be skipped over or completely ignored.

Some interesting research by Professor Colin Mason and his team at Southampton University investigated the extent to which potential business investors, or 'business angels', would read the business plans of companies seeking investment from them. Despite most business plans being at least 60 pages long, the average amount of time spent by the investor on reading the plan was eight minutes – a mere fraction of the time it would take to read it thoroughly. This is despite the large sums of money that are probably at stake. The fastest reader took just eight seconds to make up his mind.

If you are recruiting people and are sent several CVs, if you are like most people, the chances of you reading each one thoroughly are extremely remote. The normal pattern of behaviour is to seek interesting highlights and to accept or reject the CV on the basis of an impression rather than a full analysis. Although a CV is not described as a report as such, the same reading principle applies to any kind of informative document. Just as you make your mind up as to whether you like people or not in the first few seconds of meeting them, the same approach will usually apply to written information.

From the writer's perspective, it is often the case that what he or she wants to put across assumes greater emphasis than what the reader wants or needs to read. Reports are then often written 'the wrong way round' and are less effective as a result.

NLP observation

Whatever you write triggers a response of some kind. The response may be enthusiastic, apathetic or somewhere in between. It depends on the interest stimulated by the content, the sequence of that content and the language. People see the world through their own eyes and their perspectives will inevitably be different to that of the writer. The writer therefore needs to anticipate the likely responses of readers and present information accordingly.

Where there is a relatively large audience for the report or the characteristics of the recipients are not known, you should make allowance for the variation in the way people most naturally use their different senses to respond. Whether more readily stimulated by what they see, what they 'hear' (from the words in the text) or what they feel as a consequence of reading, all have a bearing on how they will respond.

Because the written word does not have the advantage of tone of voice, facial expressiveness or other forms of body language, it is comparatively limited in what it can put across. The researched data, as mentioned previously, is that in any verbal communication, 7 per cent of the meaning comes from the words themselves, 38 per cent from tone of voice and 55 per cent from body language. Thus, in any report, the capability of the words to convey information is limited to the 7 per cent, which highlights the need for those words to be succinct, accurate and unambiguous.

As UK Prime Minister Sir Winston Churchill said over half a century ago in a memo entitled 'Brevity':

> To do our work, we all have to read a mass of papers. Nearly all of them are far too long. This wastes time while energy has to be used in looking for the essential points.
>
> The aim should be reports which set out the main points in a series of short, crisp paragraphs. If a report relies on detailed analysis of some complicated factors, or on statistics, these should be set out in an appendix. Often the occasion is best addressed by submitting not a full-dress report, but an aide-memoire consisting of headings only, which can be expanded orally if needed.
>
> Let us have an end to such phrases as these: 'It is also of importance to bear in mind the following considerations' or 'Consideration should be given to the possibility of carrying into effect'. Most of these phrases are mere padding, which can be left out altogether or replaced by a single word. Let us not shrink from using the short, expressive phrase, even if it is conversational.
>
> Reports drawn up on the lines I propose may at first seem rough as compared with the flat surface of officialese jargon. But the saving in time will be great, while the discipline of setting out the real points concisely will prove an aid to clear thinking.

Although predating NLP by many years, the principles of communication are the same. Reports should be easy to understand, useful, and relevant to the reader. They should take account of the reader's ease of using them and 'do their work'. Generalizations should be avoided if they add nothing of value to meaning and there should be a balance between what is written and what is subsequently discussed.

A good pointer is to consider how reporters write their newspaper articles. The headline is to attract attention, bold text amplifies the headline and reinforces interest that in turn draws people into the piece – assuming they still remain interested. In a similar way, reports should stimulate attention, maintain interest and lead to the necessary outcome. A typical report structure could be as follows:

- Contents list
- Summary (Executive summary) – this may start with conclusions
- Introduction/Objectives/Terms of reference
  - Purpose of the report
  - Background to the report
  - Who the report is for
  - How the work was done (methodology)
  - Costs/timescales (if relevant)
  - Sources/acknowledgements
- The body of the report
- Conclusions/Recommendations
- Appendices/Annexes.

In management reports in particular, if you accept that the function of management is to manage activities, people, resources and information, it will be in the best interests of the company or organization, clients, stakeholders and employees that the reports produced confirm that objectives are being achieved and that any exceptional items are being flagged for information or decision.

What people are generally interested in includes: what has been achieved (as compared to what has merely been done); those obstacles to progress that have been identified; what has been or will be done to address such obstacles; and the specific objectives for the next period to be reported upon.

This follows closely the NLP structure of knowing your outcome, knowing how you will achieve your outcome, adaptability to changes in circumstances and a working schedule for future achievement. In this way, attention will be focused on business and organizational priorities and not dissipated on non-critical matters.

Managing events

Situation

To manage a corporate event successfully, there are a number of steps that should be followed. These are fairly standard and break down into four sections: prior to the event, in the lead up to it, during the event itself and immediately following the event. No one can organize and implement an event, whether large or small, without using an effective toolkit. The checklist that follows is something that can be adapted for general use, or amended to accommodate a special type of event. You cannot pay too much attention to detail where event organization is concerned.

Timescales for planning events vary. Some are planned at least a year in advance, while others can be put together within a few weeks. However, as a general rule it is sensible to commence your event planning as early as possible. Depending on what sort of occasion it is, you may wish to outsource aspects of the event management. For example, should it be extremely high profile, with royalty or VIP guests attending, security matters would need to be handled by experts.

The first step towards managing an event is to choose your team carefully. An event will go smoothly if everyone works well together. People who enjoy a challenge and are not afraid of working under pressure are the ones to use. These individuals should be capable of taking responsibility for whatever aspect of the project is delegated to them. Loyalty and discretion are paramount, as is attention to detail. In event management, nothing should be left to chance. It is unwise to assume things have been arranged: checking at every stage is essential.

Behaviour

Your team matters. Without them you cannot carry out your objective, which is to organize and carry out a successful event. Treat the team with respect and make it clear to them that only the highest possible standards will be acceptable. Choose individuals with whom you can work closely and harmoniously and who will do whatever it takes to deliver a result. Those who choose event management as a career thrive on high-stress environments and are cool under pressure. They are extrovert personalities and not afraid of confronting difficult situations if they arise. Assertiveness is a useful skill to possess in event management. Sometimes there isn't time to ask advice, and decisions need to be taken swiftly and put into practice immediately.

There are four stages in planning an event:

- *Stage 1:* identify the objective of the event. Is it to provide information, educate people, open a new facility or celebrate a special occasion? Early on, decide whether a speaker or VIP guest is to be invited and ensure that their diaries are clear on the proposed date. Also check that there are no major events planned that clash with the proposed event. Decide on the size of the event, optimum number of guests, scope of venue and event budget. Locate and book the venue, including any technical equipment and special items.

- *Stage 2:* work on the programme – timings, speaker, invitations, catering and hospitality. Confirm the date in writing with pivotal people: speakers, VIP guests, chairman, stakeholders and venue management. Put together a list of targeted invitees and book a photographer. Prepare the invitations and proofread publicity material carefully. Double check the wording – dates, timings and locations – prior to printing. Ensure RSVP details are clear to ensure guests respond. If security or registration is required make sure the information is clear on the invitation.

- *Stage 3:* coordinate replies to the invitations. Confirm catering arrangements with the organizers. Decide on the seating plan and other facilities, including audio-visual (AV) and technical requirements. Check all these arrangements again and confirm them in writing. Depending on the profile of the event, contact the national or technical press for coverage. Decide on the number of reserved seats you will need. Check publicity material, handouts and agendas are ready.

- *Stage 4:* on the day – check the timetable. Meet with the event management team for final instructions. Confirm their duties and what is expected of them throughout the event. At the appropriate time open the doors and greet the guests. Enjoy the occasion and at the end publicly congratulate your team on a successful outcome.

NLP observation

With regard to managing events, it is impossible not to communicate. Whether you are communicating with your events team, your specialist consultants, your invited guests, your VIPs or stakeholders, running an event is a communication process from start to finish. Whether you are deciding who to ask to make a keynote speech or what colour should be predominant in the table settings, you must communicate clearly with everyone involved.

If the meaning of your communication is the response that you get, your event should work well if you pay careful attention to the manner in which you plan and execute the event. Do not leave anything to chance. Pay great attention to detail and check and recheck every arrangement to avoid any margin for error. When people do not respond to an invitation or the take-up is slow, review what could be causing this situation. If it is something you have missed, take every possible measure to rectify the mistake or oversight before it is too late.

People have all the resources they need, it is just a question of applying them. When you choose your event management team, make sure they know what is expected of them. They are more than capable of rising to the occasion, but they must have clear instructions from you as to exactly what is required. Be scrupulous about standards but be generous with your praise. A happy team will work over and above the required hours if they know their efforts are appreciated.

Persuading others to grant your unusual or unexpected requests

Situation

Every so often you are faced with a situation where you would like to do something that others would regard as out of the ordinary. Such an example could be asking your employer for three months off next year. On the face of it, most employers would not welcome such a request, so your challenge is to put a proposition to them that makes it just as easy to say 'yes' as to say 'no' and then to ensure that 'Yes' edges it.

It would usually be a line manager to whom you would make this request and that line manager will no doubt have other staff that, given the chance, would also welcome a time off opportunity. The manager is faced with assessing the reasonableness of the request compared to the likely impact of granting it.

Behaviour

Faced with this situation, most employees, as demonstrated through practical research exercises conducted in communications courses, will set about explaining the worthiness of their reason for having the time off. They will cite their own model behaviour as employees, their commitment to the organization, a possible willingness to forego their pay for the three months, and then appeal to the heart-strings about a 'once in a lifetime opportunity' or how much better they will be as employees should the request be granted.

Most employers will be looking for an escape route that allows them to say 'no' without seeming unreasonable about it. If they can deny the request then they will avoid what they would see as the inevitable down-side consequences associated with it.

When asked to put the request in writing, the vast majority of employees will express their reasoning from their own perspective and not that of their manager. In course assessments conducted over four years with more than 300 people, most participants use the words 'I', 'me' and 'my' twice as often as they use the words 'you' or 'your'. However, there is a very good rule of thumb that says that the ratio should be the other way around.

Persuasiveness, whether it is in selling, marketing or in one-on-one transactions, is substantially enhanced by talking twice as much about 'you' and 'your' needs than about ourselves. If you have ever encountered really boring people at parties, you will have realized that it is because they insist on talking more about themselves and their interests than about you and yours.

In the situation of a manager considering this (hypothetical) request for three months' leave, the things most likely to be on his or her mind are: how the resource gap will be plugged, what colleagues will think of the decision, how other employees will react, how subsequent requests by others will be avoided if the precedent has been set, what customers might think and, as the very last factor, how the employee will feel if the answer is 'no'. The merits of the case are less important than the impact of granting the request.

NLP observation

The employer's 'map of the world' is entirely different from that of the employee and both have different sets of aims and preferences that, in the case above, are opposed.

The employee, in considering how the request can be made successful, has to change their behaviour in recognition that it is out of the ordinary and therefore disruptive to the other person. To do this needs a clear understanding of the impact of a 'yes' decision on the manager, the objections that could be made and how those objections could be countered before they are raised. Only by removing the objections systematically can there be a suitable platform for success.

The sequence involved in the process is as important as the content itself. It may be similar to the challenge of selling fridges to Eskimos. You have to think laterally in order to be able to make a compelling case, but as we know, Eskimos do buy fridges.

Managing others' anger and frustration

Situation

When someone gets upset about something, it is probably not your fault. Unfortunately you may be the person directly in their line of fire, in which case it is difficult not to feel angry and aggrieved. This is not the way to go about managing others' anger and frustration. The ability to deal with a potentially explosive situation effectively is a valuable skill and one that requires the application of certain NLP beliefs and assumptions.

It could be that you are the unfortunate recipient of someone's stored-up anger about other things which have nothing to do with the situation you're trying to sort out. Don't – whatever else you may do – take it personally. The aggrieved party will probably be eternally grateful to you for being allowed to get a lot of other things off their chest. Remember, in NLP people are not their words and behaviour.

Once you've heard the person out it is important to take back control of the situation. Explain that you wish to help solve the problem and that you will do everything you can that is within your responsibility. Remember, in NLP modifying your own behaviour can make others change theirs.

Always focus on the issue and the possible solutions, not the emotions. If the other party is abusive, repeat in a calm voice that you want to help. Explain that you can do this better if they will tell you what they want. If appropriate, call for assistance from another colleague or your superior.

Behaviour

Suppose that another member of staff or one of your customers becomes angry about something; do not respond by losing your temper too. The most important thing when dealing with someone who is angry is to find out the reason why. Is it your fault or one of your staff? Is it their own fault? Perhaps it is the result of unforeseen circumstances and no one is directly responsible.

The next thing you need to do is to listen. It's important to let the person vent their anger even if it is straight in your face. You must keep calm and show that you are sympathetic to the situation. They will (eventually) calm down. Show concern by saying things like: 'How frustrating for you', 'I can see how infuriating that must be.'

Once the person has been allowed to express their feelings and realizes that you are listening and understand their predicament, they will become (visibly) less upset. Anger is usually a short-term emotion, but unless it is released, fury will accumulate and fester. Someone who is allowed a one-sided shouting match will be more cooperative later on. Listening and acknowledging the emotion they are experiencing will help them to calm down. The bonus here is that you will have convinced them that you care.

To help you behave in an appropriate manner, draw on your own personal experiences of times when you have been confused, misunderstood or needed an answer or explanation. You can show interest by calling the person by name and letting them know that you are listening. Show empathy. In NLP terms, success depends on varying what you do until you get the result that you want – in this situation a calmer individual.

It is important to clarify the essence of the problem so that there are no misunderstandings between you and the injured party. Before taking any steps to make reparation, make sure you understand the criticism, objection, request or need. Consider the possibility of human error.

Should there be a serious problem, admit it and apologize, at once. This usually has the effect of taking the angry person entirely by surprise. It is rare for people to accept responsibility for mistakes these days.

The way to manage others' anger and frustration is best described in six steps:

1 Listen to the objection.

2 Repeat this back to the injured party to ensure there is no misunderstanding.

3 Accept responsibility for sorting out the problem.

4 Inform the person what steps you are going to take to rectify the situation.

5 Ask questions relevant to the issue.

6 Agree the steps towards reparation.

NLP observation

In terms of managing a situation, where other people's anger and frustration are concerned, do not take things personally. NLP believes that people are not their words and behaviour. Another assumption is not to think 'failure' but 'opportunity to learn'. This might not be a one-off situation, in which case a successful outcome could have positive implications for the future.

Whatever the problem, provided you can offer choice and flexibility regarding a possible solution, you will create a win–win situation. You need to establish what sort of solution will be most appropriate. Offer alternative suggestions, not just one. Success depends on varying what you do until you get the result that you want.

The bonus here is that this course of action has the effect of re-assuring the aggrieved party that they are dealing with a reasonable person. If you are sincere and sympathetic, they will be well aware that everyone can make a mistake occasionally. Remember that a positive intention motivates each behaviour. The angry person will have a positive intention by venting their frustration. They will be provoking a situation where a solution, they hope, will be forthcoming.

When managing others' anger and frustration, it is vital that the other party realizes that you are taking personal responsibility for sorting out the problem until it is resolved satisfactorily. NLP believes that people will normally make the best choice available to them in any given situation. Provided choice is available, the aggrieved party will find the best solution for him- or herself. Always identify the timescale. If the problem cannot be rectified immediately, explain how long it is likely to take. Be honest and open and you will retain control.

Communicating with people who do not immediately understand

Situation

To communicate effectively with others you must be certain that what you have transmitted has been received correctly. Whose fault is it when a communication is not understood? Is it the sender's fault or the receiver's fault? Or perhaps it is a little of each. There are endless opportunities for communication to go wrong in the workplace. Sadly, this can be a costly error – not only in terms of time, but in terms of other resources as well.

You may have to communicate with people who for one reason or another do not immediately understand. This could be because you are trying to get across a complex message. You could be attempting to implement certain changes in work processes which they do not grasp or wish to resist. There may be cultural or language differences which impede their comprehension of your communication style. Whatever the reason, if you wish to communicate effectively you must be clear and unambiguous. Your message should be simple, memorable and persuasive.

Remember that you do not immediately know whether your communication has been successfully received and understood. It is not until the people with whom you are communicating have accurately replayed your message back to you that you will find out. Getting your message across to people who do not immediately understand requires special communication skills. Every single thing you say and do has to have *impact*. The impact that you think you make may differ from the *impression* you actually make. Even more confusing is that both of these may also differ from the impression you want to make. 'I know you heard what I said, but did you understand what I meant?'

Behaviour

What you say

This is the words you use, the ideas and structure of your message. Do not use a long word when a short one will do as well. The longer the sentence, the more difficult it is to understand. Jargon should be avoided in cases where those present may not understand it. Use the active case, rather than the passive case, in speech. Positively expressed ideas are more likely to be understood clearly than those expressed negatively. For example: people sometimes use a double negative to convey a positive: 'It was not unknown for him to arrive late.' In other words, he was often late. Which one do you find easier to understand?

How you say it

Pay attention to your voice. This conveys meaning by tone, inflection, volume and pitch. If these aspects of your voice are consistent with the content of what you say, your message will be more powerful. You are also more likely to be understood in the way that you mean it.

If what you say and the way you are saying it are not aligned, the effect can be quite the reverse. Misunderstandings will occur. Remember that you must deliver a congruent message.

How you look

Your physical presence conveys meaning through your posture, your expression, your gestures and movements. If these support your message, the impact is very strong. If they undermine or contradict your message, your audience will be confused and may misunderstand you.

Your message to your audience is: 'This is the most exciting new product developed this decade.' Your vocal behaviour is a flat monotone, with lazy diction, low volume and energy. You are standing with sloppy posture and fidgeting with your pen and presentation notes. No one listening to you will believe you for one moment. Remember that your presentation and vocal behaviour speak louder than your words.

Congruence

Do you sound and look like you mean what you say? You must concentrate on delivering one single message to your listener. There is no room for mismatching of content, tone of voice and body language. For example there are many ways of saying 'Good morning'. You can come across as bored, irritated, disinterested, even sarcastic. Conversely you can be friendly, warm and approachable.

You are far more likely to achieve your objective (being understood by your audience) if you sound as though you mean what you are saying. Consider the fact that even single words can have many meanings. Think about the number of different ways of saying 'No' and 'Yes'. Depending on tone of voice, inflexion and body language these monosyllabic answers can convey a variety of different senses. Haven't you sometimes said 'yes' when you really meant to say 'no'?

Sentence lengths and their effectiveness

Table 12.1 shows the relationship between the length of sentence and the percentage of people who will understand it. Understanding decreases significantly as the length of sentence increases. If you want maximum clarity and understanding, the shorter the sentence you use the greater the number of people who will understand what you've written or said.

TABLE 12.1 Length of sentence and percentage of people who will understand it

Average length	Readability	Proportion of people who will understand
Up to 8 words	Very easy	90%
11 words	Fairly easy	85%
17 words	Standard	75%
21 words	Fairly difficult	40%
25 words	Difficult	25%
29 words or more	Very difficult	5%

NLP observation

Where clarity of communication is concerned, the most important points to remember are to be understandable, relevant, succinct and memorable. In NLP beliefs, context is what determines others' interpretation of any action or communication. Make it real, interesting and believable. With experience comes understanding; only then can you explain something well. Be sure that you have ownership of the information you are attempting to convey.

Unless you are clear about what you want to say, your audience will fail to grasp the message. Don't fall into the trap of thinking that just because you have transmitted information, you have communicated. It is wrong to assume that your audience have understood you. Should you have messed up, don't think 'failure', think 'opportunity to learn'. You can repeat your message, with better presentation skills or clearer visual aids. Do whatever it takes to make sure you are understandable and memorable. In communicating, if you use NLP skills correctly, your audience should have no room for doubt about what you are saying.

Influencing others' emotions

Situation

There may be occasions when you wish to exert influence over someone. Perhaps you are attempting to build a special relationship with a business contact. Persuasion skills are what you will need. Attempting to persuade someone to do something is a complex process. People invariably have 'their own way' of doing things and won't necessarily want to change their stance. NLP states that success depends on varying what you do until you get the result that you want.

There are many situations where you want to appeal to someone's better nature. Whether it is a straightforward business deal, or a sensitive personal matter, to be able to influence someone else's emotions you need to account for the following:

- The person with whom you are dealing is important (in their own right, to you and/or to the transaction) and should be treated as such.

- Their opinions and position will be/are respected by you (and others).

- They should feel confident that they will be dealt with sensitively, as a unique person.

- By agreeing to this exchange with you (conversation, meeting or business transaction), they should understand that there are tangible benefits available to them.

- You should explain clearly to them what the facts are and also any snags (if there are any – in most cases there usually are, and it is best to be honest about it).

- If there are compromises required, it is important to mention these at the earliest opportunity.

- You should be able to explain fluently and clearly how this arrangement can work best for both sides.

To be a convincing influencer, your approach towards the other party must be individually tailored to their viewpoint or interest. This requires preparation and should be well thought out and relevant. Communicate clearly, making your words attractive so that the other party wants to listen.

Behaviour

When seeking to persuade someone to do something, it is best to have a clearly defined purpose. You could be trying to negotiate permission to work two days a week from home. Your priority would be to convince your employer that you would get more work done if you did not have to come into the office every day of the week. You would need to explain the advantages: that your output would rise. Once your employer understands 'what's in it for them', you are on the way to achieving your objective.

Talk benefits: describe your ideas for increased working opportunities, or whatever it is that is relevant to the case in point. It is important to think this through beforehand. Every situation is different, and you may have to influence more than one person to your viewpoint: for example a board of directors or a group of partners.

If you are communicating with several people, you will not influence them unless you respect them. You must make it clear to them that you do value their opinions; show them you understand their position and that you are prepared to learn from the experience. Many business people have a healthy degree of scepticism. They could be forgiven for thinking you have a vested interest in pursuing your course of action for purely selfish reasons.

They may look for an element of 'proof'. You could provide compelling evidence, such as: 'In my last position I worked from home two days a week. During that time I was able to generate new business in several areas that I had not previously had time to research.' Perhaps it is possible to produce written proof by showing an article printed about your previous success in a professional journal. You may have a copy of a presentation you made at a conference which illustrates the sort of work you would like to undertake for them.

External evidence can be a powerful influencing tool when building credibility with another person. There may be other ways of
providing proof of your intentions, by mentioning a mutually
known contact who would be prepared to act as referee or spokes-
person on your behalf. Any way you can add value to your strategy
will be helpful. The reason for this is it will:

- help you get a better hearing;
- help improve the weight of the case you are presenting;
- possibly persuade people to act now rather than later.

NLP observation

However you choose to influence people, some methods will work
better than others. NLP beliefs state that a positive intention motivates every behaviour. You will be able to control some parts of the
process but not all. NLP beliefs also say that two people will see the
same thing in entirely different ways. Make sure you are able to see
the situation from both angles, otherwise you might not be successful.

Being flexible shows an ability to relax. Success depends on varying
what you do until you get the result you want. You may have to
compromise a little, but often 80 per cent is good enough (Pareto
principle). Whatever you are attempting to gain, if you are confident
that what you are proposing will achieve a win–win situation, keep
going. NLP states that people have all the resources they need; it is
just a question of applying them. Remain at ease with the other
party during the negotiation process. They are then likely to be
more persuadable to your way of thinking.

Dealing with difficult people face to face

Situation

Difficult people are everywhere. It just happens that sometimes you
will come face to face with someone who chooses to be unreasonable.

They may be contrary, disagreeable or disharmonious. Whatever their complaint, they won't back down and you have to deal with all of their frustrations while keeping a tight rein on your own emotions, which may be hard to do.

There are usually two main reasons why someone turns a straightforward face-to-face encounter into a war zone. You need to work out (quickly) what is going on. Otherwise the situation might deteriorate further before you can diffuse the circumstances. There could be a battle about to be waged because someone wants X when it is only possible to offer them Y.

Suppose someone is rounding on you and about to launch an attack; it is important to know what the root cause is. Is it a status battle? Are they out to prove themselves superior so they win the skirmish? It could be a battle for promotion, or another form of recognition. Are you perceived to be a threat in some way? Usually personal insecurity is at the root of this sort of problem.

Another reason for the difficult exchange could be because of territory – in other words a turf war. People are notoriously sensitive about giving up any ground, whether this is literally office space (your desk is bigger than theirs), a car park pass, a key to the director's loo or a perceived advantage in another area (your sales region is larger than theirs). Presumably the aggressive injured party is not prepared to give an inch, and resents whatever it is you have.

Almost immediately the scene is set for a 'difficult' exchange. Once you are thinking along these lines, it is very hard to change that set belief in your mind that you are dealing with an unreasonable person.

Behaviour

One of the best courses of action when faced with such a situation is to stay neutral. You should try not to dismiss the person or the situation as inevitably being unreasonable or difficult. In your mind you should not allow yourself to think 'This is going to be difficult', or 'They'll never accept what I say.' Instead, enquire what has happened, in the most cool and unemotional way you can manage.

Try to elicit why they are upset, and what needs to be done to enable them to behave differently.

Broadly speaking your aim should be to win the argument (or stand your ground) but to do it in a way that makes your colleague (opponent) feel as positive and successful as possible. After all, you can afford to be generous over small details if you've won the battle.

To start with be as pleasant and friendly as you can. Ignore any attempts to goad you with criticisms or personal insults. The nicer you can be, the less they will mind losing to you. If you fight them with a practical argument rather than an emotional outburst they will have less reason to retaliate.

The key is to win a negotiation in such a way that the other side feels they have also won. Give them as many brownie points as you can, while standing firm on the core issue. Offer them plenty of credit and praise, while making only minor concessions: 'The project you organized last year worked really well. But this year, the circumstances are different, so we need to wait until after the summer to...'

If it's a territorial matter, do not agree to their demands without making representations. If a solution is desirable, suggest trading territory with other responsibilities. This will work if these responsibilities are prestigious. 'If I concede this region to you, it will free me up for some other tasks.' There is no need to explain that these tasks include high-level negotiations with key stakeholders. That is your trade-off and they are not interested in you.

The chances are that the antagonist will be so pleased to have 'won' something from the encounter, they will not realize that what they are gaining is not all that significant. You would be wise to continue in your neutral but pleasant way and let them think that they have got the better of you.

NLP observation

NLP states that people are not their words and behaviour. This is why, in difficult face-to-face encounters, it is essential that you get to the root cause of the disagreement as soon as possible. The aggressive behaviour on the part of the antagonist is probably a cover for their feeling of insecurity.

People respond according to their internal maps of reality. Their map and your map are not congruent. It is probably going to be impossible for the two of you to read from the same map. So fold your map away, and let them rant on about whatever grievance they feel is most urgent.

If people normally make the best choice available to them in any given situation, you will end up with a win–win situation in this encounter. As described in the 'Behaviour' section above, you are letting go of something in order to regain something far more valuable. But the other party is so pleased to have 'won' that they are unconcerned about the importance of your trade-off.

Dealing with difficult people on the phone

Situation

Your job, as a good communicator and NLP practitioner, is to get your message across to people and for it to be received clearly. Sometimes, however, misunderstandings occur and resentment can result. People fight against things they consider unreasonable. Fighting takes up time and uses energy. The effort involved impairs performance and motivation evaporates.

Considering how complex communication and behaviour can be, it is not surprising that sometimes things go wrong. If you encounter a problem, you probably have no difficulty in convincing yourself that it is not your fault. In other words you 'externalize' the issue – it becomes someone else's error. The ownership then passes to them and away from you. This is what is happening when you come up against difficult people. Sometimes there is a genuine grievance – 'My order did not arrive on Monday, and you promised it would.' Other times it is because information has been misunderstood, or because there is an emotional reaction that has no logic – your girlfriend has just told you the relationship is over, so you ring your bank and shout at the customer services assistant about your bank charges being extortionate.

Such problems, challenges or difficult situations are usually genuine for the person in their predicament. For you, the receiver of the behaviour, the challenge is not to react in a negative way too. It is natural in the face of a verbal attack to defend yourself by getting angry back. But the best way of avoiding an argument is not to enter into one.

Behaviour

Confrontation is sometimes inevitable, but should you be unfortunate enough to receive a call and find the other party already on fire, here are some things you can do. First, welcome the disagreement and thank the other party for pointing out the problem. Distrust your first instinctive impression ('Here's a complete idiot – why did I pick up this call?'). Control your temper – remember it takes two to have an argument. Listen first, and keep listening. The caller will (eventually) stop ranting. Look for any areas of agreement. Be honest, promise to study the caller's complaint carefully. Thank them for bringing the matter to your attention. Postpone reaction (or offering an immediate solution) to give both sides time to reflect.

> Control your temper – remember it takes two to have an argument

It is important that when someone is shouting, you should be silent and listen. If two people are shouting, there is no communication. But in NLP it is impossible not to communicate something. You just won't reach an agreement this way. Show respect for other people's opinions – never tell them they are wrong. All they really want to know is that you understand there is a problem and you're going to do something about it.

Start the dialogue by suggesting that perhaps they are right. You could say: 'I could be wrong here. I'd prefer to be right, but let's look at the facts.' Using diplomacy can turn the tide of a heated exchange. Be brave enough to admit you are wrong, if the facts determine that it is so.

You can always use kindness and courtesy to help things along – remember the fable about the sun making you take your coat off more quickly than the wind? Gentleness and friendliness often achieve far more than fury and force.

If you deal with people in this way, every situation should have a solution. Your ability to respond in a flexible and responsible way will work wonders. Success in dealing with difficult people on the phone depends on your getting a sympathetic grasp of the other person's viewpoint. You cannot see them, all you have to go on is the tone of their voice. (But this is a lot easier than dealing with someone who has written a nasty letter.)

NLP observation

By using good communications skills in the workplace you can defuse difficult situations. Verbal communication (taking telephone calls in this particular instance) requires 100 per cent responsibility by the person involved. When communicating on the phone be aware of your own personality as well as the other party's. Two people see things in entirely different ways and people respond according to their own maps of reality. You will succeed if you give clear messages and signals, but be flexible as to your approach, because you may need more than one attempt before a resolution is achieved.

Dealing with difficult people in written correspondence

Situation

If you are in the position of having to deal with awkward people on a regular basis (because your job as Customer Relationship Manager carries this responsibility) you need a well-planned strategy to help you. Whether you are communicating with people face to face, over the telephone or in written form, there are some standard rules that apply in all cases. Difficult people have the ability to be difficult under any circumstances – possibly because they are angry and frustrated and 'demand satisfaction'. Your 'response toolkit' should be organized so that it will work in every case. It will simply need to be appropriately adapted to fit the individual circumstances you are dealing with.

Whether you are dealing with an angry boss, customer, supplier, member of staff or a friend, you must be clear about what you are trying to do. The channel of communication you choose can influence greatly the success or failure of getting your message across. Sometimes people choose the wrong channel of communication and then wonder why they get an unwelcome response. If you choose to reply to an awkward person in writing, you must consider carefully what you are going to say. It is often easier to deal with difficult people on a face-to-face basis. The personal touch can have a soothing effect. But assuming you have been asked to write someone a letter, remember that written communication is more difficult than a face-to-face exchange. This is because it is two-dimensional. You have no control over the reader's reaction. The last thing you need in dealing with a difficult person is to upset them further by the use of ill-judged words or phrases – whether that is a sarcastically worded letter or a furious e-mail dashed off in the heat of the moment. Something written in black and white that leaps off the page can turn a problem into a disaster. Two people see the same thing in entirely different ways and in written communication misconstrued meaning must be avoided.

The purpose of written communication (whatever form it takes) is to convey facts. When dealing with people who are upset, you must detach emotion from your response. If you can write exactly what you want, succinctly, effectively and expressing your side of the matter without heat or rancour, you will have achieved your objective. Hopefully this will elicit a measured response from the recipient. To help you with similar situations, or if it is a serious matter and could lead to disciplinary action, it is important to keep a record of the following: (1) the party with whom you were communicating; (2) the purpose of the communication; (3) a copy of the means by which it took place – e-mail/letter/fax; and (d) the response or outcome.

Behaviour

The best way of communicating in writing with difficult people is to make the other person feel important and respected. NLP is all about knowing how to modify behaviour to achieve a desired outcome. The desire of fellow human beings to be appreciated can be likened to an ongoing hunger. It is a craving that is not satisfied. When dealing with angry or dissatisfied people, if you can assuage this craving you will have the art of successful communication well and truly within your grasp. Remember that in NLP a positive intention motivates every behaviour. Perhaps the difficult person doesn't want to be difficult, they are just so frustrated that they can't be polite at this particular moment.

The next thing to do is to avoid criticizing the person in your correspondence. This will serve only to make matters (which are already bad enough) even worse. Belittling people, being unkind, kills off any possibility of reaching a swift and conciliatory conclusion. Most people will respond better and put more effort into finding a solution to differences if you adopt a tone of approval in your communication. If you can go so far as to praise them for taking the time to write and draw your attention to such an important matter this is even better. You will – at a stroke – have removed the necessity for them to keep their gun pointed towards you. It costs very little to deal with people in a courteous, polite and compassionate manner, even under the most troublesome circumstances.

People are usually only interested in what they want. Angry people demand satisfaction – rather in the way that duellists asked someone to meet them at dawn with drawn swords. So one of the best ways of dealing with a difficult person in correspondence is to ask (if they haven't already told you) what they want. The successful troubleshooter arouses a desire in the other side to seek a resolution. If you can find out what the other person's viewpoint is, and see things from that angle, you can then work out a strategy for obtaining a solution to the impasse.

Here are a few tips for writing etiquette:

- Don't just reply by e-mail because it's easy: use whichever format is most appropriate.

- Never use CAPITAL LETTERS. This is rude and it looks as if you are shouting.
- Don't put something in writing that is confidential – it will be abused.
- Don't fire off a response while you are angry (this applies equally to letter or e-mail).
- Always check your spelling and punctuation – errors can and will occur.
- Keep your reply as short as possible – don't use unnecessary words or meaningless phrases.
- Be polite: use the correct salutation, address the person by name and use their title.
- Use attachments or enclosures if further clarity (or documentary evidence) is needed.
- Copy correspondence only to relevant concerned parties (your boss, their solicitor).

NLP observation

Your job, as a skilled communicator, is to get your message across to someone in writing and for it to be received willingly and understood. Go back to the basic method for establishing good rapport with someone – the creation of trust, instilling confidence, being positive, prepared to take criticism and feedback, mirroring their feelings. 'I am writing to you because I was so upset to hear that you had been let down by our company...'

In NLP a positive intention motivates every behaviour. In writing to someone who is being difficult, try to determine what caused the problem and you will then be in a position to seek a satisfactory resolution.

Effective presentations

Situation

Presentations take place in organizations everywhere, day in, day out. They can cover such things as press briefings and training sessions, to canvass support or to inform about proposed changes. They could also be speeches at conferences, a retirement party or to welcome a new member of staff. Whatever the reason for them, the important thing is to be clear and understandable. The remark attributed to the late ex-US President Nixon sums this up: 'I know that you understand what you think I said, but I am not sure that you realize that what you heard is not what I meant.' Now do you see what I mean?

Behaviour

The golden rule for all presenters is to imagine that they are in the audience. How helpful this advice is. Because you have probably sat through far too many bad presentations, the last thing you want to do is be responsible for creating another one. Aim not at being understood but at being impossible to misunderstand. There is advice elsewhere in the book that is relevant here – on personal presentation, use of body language, eyes, voice, breathing, as well as choice of vocabulary and other things – which will not be repeated here. But there are three important things to remember:

- Hearing – this is rarely 100 per cent, not because half your audience are deaf but because people's concentration wanders. Your audience, however polite, can't concentrate fully for long periods of time.

- Message dilution – even if people hear exactly what you say they dilute the message through their own personal filters (experience, knowledge, expectations, prejudices, values). There is also an optimum number of points that people can remember – usually no more than five.

- Conclusion – this may be drawn by the audience before the full impact of the presentation has been made. This is a difficult situation to reverse, so it pays to give a summary of the presentation at the beginning.

A clear intention helps you to present well. Do you want to inform people of something? Are you giving the presentation to instruct or explain, motivate or persuade? Perhaps you wish to prompt a debate about an important issue? Or are you demonstrating something – by means of modelling or trialling?

You also need objectives: some background to what you are talking about is always useful. An explanation of why the presentation is necessary. Exactly what is happening and the effects it is likely to have on individuals, the organization and/or the industry or profession as a whole.

Finally, what action needs to be taken, by whom and by when? Composing the material, and arranging the presentation comes next. This part of the preparation is crucial to its successful delivery. Decide what you want to say, then list every point (without worrying about sequence or structure). Sort all the ideas you have written down into some logical order, recording the sequence in which you will talk about things and how each point relates to the other. Now you need to arrange them in the precise way they connect to the topic.

You should now have your rough notes sorted into a list and rewritten in an orderly form. This can then be subjected to a final review to ensure that you are not trying to say too much, or too little, and that each point you make is of equal importance. There may need to be a little fine-tuning, but, depending on experience, this can be done quite quickly.

You are now able to produce a set of speaker's notes. You can also at this point prepare any visual aids you might need. They do help in lots of ways but you cannot depend on them entirely and thus avoid preparation. The notes could be purely for your own use, to accompany a slide presentation or be distributed to the audience at the end as a handout. Now all you have to do is to rehearse your presentation, arrive at the (correct) venue, in good time and deliver your speech. Simple, isn't it?

When giving a presentation it is sensible advice to expect the unexpected. What does this mean? Unforeseen incidents – dropping your notes, technology letting you down (no microphone, the PowerPoint presentation refuses to load onto the computer), low-flying aircraft, fire alarms ringing, someone faints or falls backwards off the stage. (This has happened in the presence of this chapter's writer, but not to her personally.)

The dilemma here is how best to deal with the unexpected occurrence. Adopting the right attitude helps a great deal. Accept that things can and will go wrong (occasionally) even for those best prepared. Acknowledge the incident (there's no point in pretending that nothing has happened). Consider your options (you announce you'll take a break while the situation is recovered). Decide on the chosen course of action (if the building is on fire, you will have to follow standard procedures and leave). Communicate (tell people what is happening). Resume or abandon, depending on the circumstances.

NLP observation

In order to come across well, remember to respect your audience – and they will give you a better hearing as a result. The checklist is as follows:

- Content. Make it clear and understandable. Decide the level of detail and technicality. Assemble points in logical sequence, link to visual aids. Make it relevant to your audience.

- Structure. Arrange contents clearly with defined objectives. Decide direction, use signposts. Start with the end in mind, give indication of what is to come. Make sure there is continuity and linked progression. Pay attention to timing.

- Maintenance of interest. Focus on the audience; be enthusiastic. Show examples – illustrations, visual aids, humour, anecdotes. Involve the audience, include question and answer session if appropriate (or time allows).

NLP states that context is what determines others' interpretation of any action or communication. Take care to ensure your audience understands the purpose you have in mind when giving your presentation. Only by doing this will they get the meaning of your communication and be able to respond to it appropriately.

Selling: the consultative approach

Situation

Consultative selling involves deeper questioning and interaction with the potential customer, particularly in a business context. This can include organizational and operational matters, and can extend beyond the merits just of the product or service itself. It seeks to understand the implications of the purchase.

This leads to greater understanding by the questioner of the other's wider needs, and the questioning process itself also results in a greater trust, rapport and empathy between salesperson and buyer. It leads to a situation where a purchase is more likely to be made on its perceived value and not on price alone.

Part of the process of selling is to uncover needs in buyers that they had not previously articulated despite their potential payback value. In so-called 'needs-creation' selling, the salesperson seeks to identify and then highlight a particular need, problem, challenge or issue that a potential customer might face. This assumes that the supplier organization is able to offer a suitably matched remedy or solution (product and/or service proposition) once the needs are firmly established in the buyer's mind.

The consultative aspect exists in the salesperson's ability, experience and expertise, to 'consult' with the buyer in developing a solution.

Behaviour

Many people think that selling is something you do to people, when it should more properly be regarded as creating a valuable opportunity to purchase. 'Don't sell to me, let me buy', is a good way of looking at it.

In research conducted a number of years ago, according to UK sales recruitment and training company Metamorphosis, over 60 per cent of second-year undergraduates in the United States, when questioned, said that they would consider a career in sales. The equivalent survey of second-year British undergraduates resulted in just 4 per cent saying they would consider it.

This illustrates what seems, in the British mindset, to be an inherent mistrust of salespeople in a profession that requires considerable skill and, ultimately, integrity. It is also worth noting that British universities rarely, if at all, offer degree courses in selling. This is a surprising gap considering that so much of the economy depends on selling goods and services effectively. The stereotypes of secondhand car salesmen and estate agents do nothing to enhance the status of what is a perfectly honourable and legitimate profession.

In the United Kingdom in particular, successful selling depends to a great extent on applying principles that are inherent in NLP philosophy.

NLP observation

In just seven to ten seconds of meeting someone, you make up your mind whether you are going to like that person or not. You form an immediate opinion based on what you sense and observe. It is a truism that people buy from people. The challenge, therefore, is to establish rapport as your first priority in the selling process. Rapport governs all aspects of NLP and is the basis on which all good communication can flow.

Part of establishing rapport is in mirroring the other person's tone, posture and behavioural traits; in other words going along with the way the other person is. It is only by doing this and effectively getting someone 'on-side' that you create for yourself the opportunity to lead the conversation in the way that you want to. The essence of good salesmanship is being able to lead in a way that induces others to follow.

This also requires flexibility and the preparedness to change an approach until it dovetails with the state of mind of the potential customer. This flexibility is necessary because of the different ways people prefer to receive information and takes account of visual, aural and emotional receptors that most prevail. When selling to groups, being aware of different roles and sensing preferences will help manage the process of being inclusive and with a greater likelihood of success.

Negotiation principles

Situation

Negotiation, whether in selling or in any other activity, aims to create a situation where both parties will be satisfied with the outcome. Negotiation is a form of collaboration that leads to mutually acceptable results. For a negotiation to be successful in a sales situation depends on the neutral status of both buyer and seller. An adversarial approach does not make for a mutually acceptable conclusion.

You are in the best negotiating position when you have the freedom of choice and are in a position to withdraw if you need to. If the result is too important to you, your negotiating position will be weakened.

If you are selling a product, service or simply an idea, you will do so more effectively with a big picture as compared to detail. The opposite is true of the buyer who achieves the best outcome by negotiating on an item-by-item basis. This also holds true when putting an argument where a big idea is deconstructed on an item-by-item basis.

A mistake in negotiating is to make concessions that are unnecessary and offered too early. In NLP terms you should always aim for the best outcome.

Behaviour

If you regard negotiation as a challenge involving winners and losers, you are more likely to end up a loser. This is particularly the case against a good negotiator, who will have calculated a situation where you think you have won but have been lulled into that position on a false premise. We all know politicians who, when defeated, have claimed a particular result as a victory when everyone else knows that it was nothing of the sort.

A particular illustration of this involves an ancient game called the Prisoners' Dilemma (see explanation of how to play this at the end of this section), based on a situation where two prisoners were facing a death sentence unless they could answer certain questions correctly. The outcome could be that one or other would be set free, both would be set free or both would be executed. The optimum outcome depends on collaboration rather than the perceived need to win.

Negotiation often exposes a whole gamut of behaviours usually designed to put one party at an advantage against the other. Tone of voice, use of the eyes, pace of speech, gestures, posture and other uses of speech and body language are often used to strengthen one's own position at the expense of the other.

There are also legitimate ploys in, for example a sales situation, where it is usually a good idea to let the other side go first. Also, rather than give concessions for no particular return, it is better to trade them for something in return.

Negotiation can be a hotbed of generalizations, distortions and deliberate misinterpretations, which is why a neutral starting point and mutually agreed goals make the whole process so much more effective. Buyers can defer to a higher authority as a delaying tactic or seek more time 'to examine the facts'. It is essential to have researched and to be fully conversant with all the elements of the buyer's needs, including those of the different people involved in making a decision. This enables you to maintain the strength of your own negotiating position.

NLP observation

If you are not clear about what success criteria you expect, it is unlikely that you will get the most satisfactory result, as the process of negotiation cannot have been properly planned.

The other party to the negotiation will have started with an entirely different perceptual position to yours, so it is important to work towards converging the two positions. Be prepared to adapt your behaviour in order to achieve that convergence.

If you encounter resistance, it is unlikely that you have established the level of rapport needed to be fully trusted in your propositions. Through better mirroring of behaviour and use of language, and asking the right questions, you will help create more confidence in your negotiating integrity.

CASE STUDY Prisoners' Dilemma: a negotiation game for two groups

The objective is for your group to end up with a positive score.*

Procedure

The organizer will visit your group and ask you to decide whether to play red or to play blue. (He/she will not tell you which colour the other group has played.)

When both groups have made their move, the organizer will announce the colours that have been played and these are scored as follows:

FIGURE 12.1

IF GROUP 1 PLAYS:	IF GROUP 2 PLAYS:	THEN GROUP 1 SCORES:	THEN GROUP 2 SCORES:
RED	RED	+3	+3
RED	BLUE	−6	+6
BLUE	RED	+6	−6
BLUE	BLUE	−3	−3

There will be ten rounds.

After the fourth round the organizer will ask the groups whether they would like a conference. This conference will only take place at the request of both groups. If either does not wish to confer, then no meeting will take place.

After the eighth round there will be a second opportunity for a conference should both groups wish.

The ninth and tenth rounds score double.

---

* The usual outcome of teams undertaking the above exercise is that the objective has been wrongly interpreted and the concept of win–win will have been ignored – but there are occasional exceptions!

Where to find out more about NLP and NLP facilities

There are very many sources of information about NLP and anyone following up is well advised to research their provenance as they come from a number of different angles.

However, as well as the many books on the subject, the following contacts may be useful:

The Association of NLP (ANLP)
41 Marlowes
Hemel Hempstead
Herts
HP1 1LD
Tel: 0845 053 1162
www.anlp.org

International NLP Trainers Association
PO Box 187
Gosport
PO12 9AE
www.inlpta.com

Professional Guild of NLP
PO Box 104
Clitheroe
BB7 9ZG
Tel: 0845 226 7334
www.professionalguildofnlp.com

The Society of NLP
www.purenlp.com
(founded 30 years ago in the USA)

www.businessballs.com
(very useful reference source)

www.nlpconnections.com
(forum and free resources)

www.nlpdevelopment.org.uk
(a networking hub)

www.nlpevents.co.uk
(very comprehensive list of UK events)

www.nlpresearch.org
(Surrey University)

www.nlpuniversitypress.com
(encyclopedia)

www.nlpworld.com
(publication and good source of information)

www.ppi-nlp-store.com
(an NLP bookstore)

Wikipedia also has useful and interesting background details and explanations.

Glossary

With the exception of a few of them, this glossary contains basic NLP terms that have not been included in the book. There are many more NLP terms in addition to these and further definitions and terminology can easily be found on the internet.

We have made a cross-reference of the terms shown as they relate to particular sections in the book and the meanings can therefore be inferred through those texts. All have been covered or their meanings alluded to.

Anchor – a link with something that stimulates a response; such as a dog salivating when it hears a bell, or someone sweating at the sight of a hypodermic syringe. 10, 71–72, 121–32

Auditory – information that you pick up with your ears. Also linked with *visual, kinaesthetic, gustatory* and *olfactory* (sight, feeling, taste and smell). 45–46, 63–65

Away from (cf *towards*) – this indicates someone's tendency to move in the opposite way to their preferred logical preference. This is a negative as compared to a positive tendency. 46–47, 156

Calibration – this is working out through reading others' unconsciously projected signals, the true state of their mind and therefore your approach to them. 16–17, 59, 75–76

Chunking – expressing or reading information in bigger or smaller pieces so as to match the other person's needs or intentions. A chunking difference would be explaining the function of a catalytic converter when the person purchasing the car is more interested in the look and smell of its red leather seats. 33, 35, 74, 177–82, 210

Congruence – the genuine alignment of words, tone, verbal pace and volume, gestures and body language. 11, 60, 73, 192, 205–07

Conscious competence – this is where a skill you are acquiring is fully there but not automatic. You have not yet turned it into a habit, such as, for example, changing gear when learning to drive a car. 11, 43–44

Conscious incompetence – this precedes conscious competence and is when you know what you have to do but do not yet have the skill to do it. 11, 43–44

Context – is what conveys the received meaning of what you communicate. Whistling in the face of danger would be seen as a sign of fear and not cheerfulness. 8, 9, 17–18, 21

Deletion – this is where you consciously or unconsciously ignore aspects of a communication that someone might have with you. 13, 42, 196–97, 199–201, 201–02

Elicitation – the process of discovering what is going on in someone's mind. 10, 16–17, 208–13

Epistemology – an academic discipline that seeks to show how much we know about our own knowledge and knowledge processes. 77–78, 90–91, 121–32

Eye accessing cues – these are NLP's standard way of interpreting lateral eye movements to denote visual, auditory or kinaesthetic contemplation. They are said, for example, to indicate thoughtfulness, dishonesty, memories or concern as compared with others to indicate what the person might be thinking. Different eye directions denote, for example, honesty, thoughtfulness, dishonesty, etc. 62–63

Frame – the particular perception you might have because of your individual frame of reference. What you perceive as compared to what is. 11, 27, 41, 42–43, 188

Future pacing – practising something in your mind that you will later enact with greater assurance of doing it as you want to. 121–32

Generalization – applying a simplification of speech or meaning so as to aid or thwart understanding. 14, 80–82, 136

Gustatory – of the taste glands. 45–46

Incongruence – confused and maybe conflicting internal signals and outward behaviour in the face of uncertainty of wishes. 21, 129, 196–97

Kinaesthetic – to do with touch and also emotional feelings. Goes with *auditory* and *visual* preferences for giving or receiving information. 45–46

Leading – having established rapport, you can then influence someone in the direction you want because of the atmosphere of trust that has been built. 28, 47, 48, 50, 92–111, 112–20, 132, 185–86

Matching – copying other people's posture, tone, mannerisms and so on for the purpose of building rapport. 92–111

Meta language – this is a higher level of language that summarizes or can be used to disguise meaning. It is frequently used by all of us but notably by politicians. 13, 74, 79, 82, 87, 157

Meta model – this includes meta language and also covers the way we delete, distort and generalize language. It also includes the questions that could be asked in order to clarify meaning in the face of such language. 73, 80, 82, 84, 87

Metaphor – stories, analogies and parables used to illustrate another situation. 'Raining stair rods' would be an example. 75, 122

Mirroring – matching aspects of someone else's language, accent, tone or behaviour. 11, 58, 62

Mismatching – deliberately behaving contrary to the other person in order to reduce or remove rapport. 135–37, 155, 159

Modal operators – your own standards by which you judge others' and your own words and behaviour. 8, 19–20, 37, 49, 88, 187

Model of the world – the world as you see it. 9, 23, 24, 149

Modelling – emulating the behaviour and habits of effective people. 58–59, 121

Olfactory – to do with the sense of smell. 45–46, 57

Pacing – a means, through emulation, of rapidly establishing rapport. 75, 99–111

Perceptual filters – our own background and experience that shapes the way we react to the world, people and situations. 16–17, 25, 29–30, 40–41, 66, 71, 162–68

Phonological ambiguity – words that sound the same but are spelled differently. 17–18, 30–31

Preferred thinking style – thinking in pictures, words or tangible experiences as best suits your personality type. 45–46, 146–47, 209–10

Presuppositions – beliefs or assumptions that underpin NLP principles. 8, 9, 16–36, 49

Rapport – establishment of the emotional basis for a good relationship. 11, 74–75, 92–111, 139–40, 204

Representational systems – your five senses. 45–46, 67, 147

Requisite variety – your ability to make changes to thought and behaviour in order to achieve a previously established goal. 26, 27, 28, 31–32, 34, 36, 40, 47, 49–50, 55, 132, 137, 143, 173–74, 203

Sensory acuity – perceptiveness. 61, 175–77, 196, 209

Stimulus Response Associationist theory – a principle of learning through the proxy of another experience. 68, 69, 121–32

Sub-modalities – extensions to the five senses where we can, for example, apply colour to shape rather than just see shape on its own. 45–46

Towards (cf *away from*) – people are positively inclined to do the things necessary to achieve their goals. 46–47

Trance – diversion of the mind to a different focal point and leading to otherwise hard-to-achieve outcomes. Group behaviour, if untrue to your values, can induce you to behave out of character. 37–38, 52, 53, 68

Unconscious competence – the development of a habit in performing certain actions so that you are not conscious of doing them. It's why you cannot sometimes remember driving the last few miles. 11, 15, 43–44

Unconscious incompetence – before learning to drive, not being aware of how badly you will cope the first time you are behind a wheel. It is a natural precursor to the learning process. 11, 15, 43–44

Visual mode – the complement to *auditory* and *kinaesthetic* preferred sensory styles. 45–46

Further reading

For those who want to go into more specific behaviour affecting the setting up, running, and making money from a business is *The Effective Entrepreneur* (ISBN 978 1 905823 22 2). Author and NLP practitioner and business coach John Caines has run a number of very successful businesses and currently chairs a regional investment group. The authors are grateful to John for his help and wisdom in supporting the demystification process behind *Understanding NLP*.

For further information on communications skills *Effective Business Writing* (ISBN 978 0 7494 5453 1) written by Patrick Forsyth and published by Kogan Page is helpful. Patrick Forsyth runs Touchstone Training & Consultancy, which advises on marketing, management and communication skills. An established author, he has written many successful business books including *Successful Time Management, How to Motivate People* and *How to Write Reports and Proposals* (all part of the Creating Success series published by Kogan Page).

Further reading

Index

acronyms 126–27
actions, varying 26, 104–07, 107–10
adapt, human race 25
aides memoires 127–29
ambiguity 18
anchoring 10
anger, management of in
    others 187–90
angry 24
approaches, different 103–11
argue 14
attitude 34
assertiveness, skills of 158–61
  control of 49
audiences 35

behaviour 16, 19–20, 42
  during meetings 144–45
  ego states 47–49
  mind and its effects on 37–55
  odd 24
blame 34
body, impact on communication
    56–66
body language 19, 56–63, 65–66
bullying 50, 135–37
business strategy, types of 122–23
bystander effect 53

capabilities to widen your skills range
    175–213
change 25–29
character types 103–05
choices 25
Cinderella factor and NLP 155–57
cognitive dissonance 130
collaborative learning 123–25
communication 35
  clear 190
  effectiveness 112–20
  good 13
  poor 13
  verbal 165–67
competence, learning 43
complaints 34

conscious mind 12, 42
confidence 112–13
  in own abilities 162–65
conflicting ideas 129–30
contact, personal 92–117
context 17, 35
  unambiguous 18
control
  over actions 38
  over mind 38
curiosity 106

deletion 13
difficult people
  face to face 196
  on the phone 199
  in correspondence 201
distort, information 13

ego states 47–49
emotions 11
  influencing others 194
emphasis 18
encounters, face-to-face 92–106
events, management of 182
experience 33
eye contact 62–63

failure 34
false positions 14
filters 35

generalisation 14
  advantages, disadvantages
    80–83
goal 32
group behaviour, dynamics 52
guesswork 131

hearing 45
hypnotism 68

ideas
  conflicting 129
  development of 141–43

immune system   19
impact of language   88–91
improvement, personal   34
incompetence, learned   43
incongruous speech   39
influencing skills   112–19
influencing others' emotions   194
inhibited   35
instant messaging   59
interpersonal skills   94–97, 107–11
interpretation   17, 23–24
interviews   175–77

language, coded   13
  decoding   79
  direct, indirect   81–82
  distorting truth   82–83
  Greek influence   90–91
  learning   31
  loaded   14
  meaning and understanding
    79–81
  power of   88–91
  recall   73–76
  unhelpful   13
  word choice   130
learn   34
learning
  aid   15
  by association   68–69, 125–26
  effective   121–24
  field cognition   125
  styles of   121–30

management
  alignment   141–43
  poor   138–40
managers, language   34
managing
  anger in others   187–90
  by objectives   138
  events   182
  teams and projects   145
  time in others   152–54
  your own time   168–70
map   23
McGregor, Douglas   149
meetings, conduct at   143–45
memory, recall   76, 83, 88–90
memoires, aides   126–29
mental attitudes   19, 49

messaging, instant   59
metaphorical path   32
mind
  and body   19
  conscious   12, 42–43
  effects on behaviour   37, 49–50
  openers, exercises   41–42
  retention of information   39
  unconscious   42–43
mindset, limited   40
mirroring   11, 58
misinterpretation   17–18
misunderstandings, eliminate
    30–31
mnemonics   126
modelling   11, 58
modifying behaviour   28
motivation   147–51

NLP
  basic techniques   10–11
  beliefs   8–9, 16
  building blocks   7
  challenges, management   133–74
  definition   1–2
  external factors   10
  internal factors   10
  nervous system   71–72
  origins   2
  outcomes   7
  presuppositions   16
  and Shakespeare   37
  situations you may face   135–74
  the 'Cinderella' factor   155–57
negative thinking   46–48
negotiation principles   210–12
negotiation tactics   113–14
nervous system   67–72
  technical aspects   69–70
neurotransmitters   19

O'Keeffe, John   41
open mind   40
operational principles, NLP   8
opportunities
  creating   117–19
  for personal development   158

pause, power of   114
perception   23
personal strengths   66

personality 12
persuasion
    art of 112
    techniques 185
phobias 12
positive
    intention 19–20
    thinking 46–47
presentation skills 72
presentations, effective 205–07
project management 145–47
psychology, language 13

rapport 11, 62, 92–111
    insufficient 35
reactions – people and situations
    53–54
reality, interpretation 23, 24
receptiveness to change 170–74
reflecting and summarising 166
reframing 11
relationship building skills 92–111
report writing 177–82
resources, people's 31–32

seeing 45
self-knowledge 50–51

selling, the consultative approach
    208–10
smile 66
spelling 77–78
stress 19
summarizing and reflecting 166

thinking, negative and positive 46–47
time management
    of others 152–55
    personal 168–70
touching and feeling 46
training 33
transactional analysis 47–48
trial and error learning 125
two-to-one ratio 75

unconscious mind 12, 42–43
understanding 33

verbal
    ambiguity 18
    communication 165–67
vocal skills 63–65

workplace situations 32
writing reports 177–82

The European Superpower

Also by John McCormick

COMPARATIVE POLITICS IN TRANSITION

CONTEMPORARY BRITAIN

ENVIRONMENTAL POLICY IN THE EUROPEAN UNION

THE EUROPEAN UNION: POLITICS AND POLICIES

THE GLOBAL ENVIRONMENTAL MOVEMENT

UNDERSTANDING THE EUROPEAN UNION A Concise Introduction

The European Superpower

John McCormick

First published 2007 by
PALGRAVE MACMILLAN
Houndmills, Basingstoke, Hampshire RG21 6XS and
175 Fifth Avenue, New York, N. Y. 10010
Companies and representatives throughout the world

PALGRAVE MACMILLAN is the global academic imprint of the Palgrave
Macmillan division of St. Martin's Press, LLC and of Palgrave Macmillan Ltd.
Macmillan® is a registered trademark in the United States, United Kingdom
and other countries. Palgrave is a registered trademark in the European
Union and other countries.

ISBN-13: 978–1–4039–9845–3   hardback
ISBN-10: 1–4039–9845–0   hardback
ISBN-13: 978–1–4039–9846–0   paperback
ISBN-10: 1–4039–9846–9   paperback

This book is printed on paper suitable for recycling and made from
fully managed and sustained forest sources.
Logging, pulping and manufacturing processes are expected to conform
to the environmental regulations of the country of origin.

A catalogue record for this book is available from the British Library.

A catalog record for this book is available from the Library of Congress.

10	9	8	7	6	5	4	3	2
16	15	14	13	12	11	10	09	08

Printed and bound in China